GREAT WRITING

KB188297

FIFTH EDITION
Keith S. Folse
April Muchmore-Vokoun
Elena Vestri

NATIONAL GEOGRAPHIC
LEARNING

Australia · Brazil · Mexico · Singapore · United Kingdom · United States

National Geographic Learning,
a Cengage Company

Great Writing 1: Great Sentences for Great Paragraphs
Keith S. Folse

Publisher(Asia): Andrew Robinson
Sr. Regional Director, Asia ELT/School: Michael Cahill
Publishing Manager: Lauren Kim

© 2025 Cengage Learning, Inc.

WCN: 03-300-327-1020-782

ALL RIGHTS RESERVED. No part of this work covered by the copyright herein may be reproduced or distributed in any form or by any means, except as permitted by U.S. copyright law, without the prior written permission of the copyright owner.

"National Geographic", "National Geographic Society" and the Yellow Border Design are registered trademarks of the National Geographic Society ® Marcas Registradas

For product information and technology assistance, contact us at
Cengage Learning Korea Customer & Sales Support, NGLKorea.co.kr

For permission to use material from this text or product,
submit all requests online at **cengage.com/permissions**
Further permissions questions can be emailed to
permissionrequest@cengage.com

ISBN: 979-8-214-50232-8

National Geographic Learning
200 Pier 4 Boulevard
Boston, MA 02210
USA

Cengage Learning Korea Ltd
14F, YTN Newsquare
76 Sangamsan-ro, Mapo-gu
Seoul, 03926, Korea

Locate your local office at **international.cengage.com/region**

Printed in Korea
Print Number: 01 Print Year: 2025

CONTENTS

GREAT WRITING MAKES GREAT WRITERS

The new edition of *Great Writing* provides clear explanations, academic writing models, and focused practice to help students write great sentences, paragraphs, and essays. Every unit has expanded vocabulary building, sentence development, and more structured final writing tasks.

National Geographic images and content spark students' imaginations and inspire their writing.

Each unit includes:

PART 1: Elements of Great Writing teaches the fundamentals of writing.

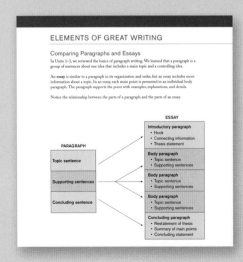

Writing Models encourage students to analyze and use the features of great writing in their own work.

Targeted Grammar presents clear explanations and examples that students can immediately apply to their work.

PART 2: **Building Better Vocabulary** highlights academic words, word associations, collocations, word forms, and vocabulary for writing.

New Words to Know boxes throughout each unit target carefully-leveled words students will frequently use.

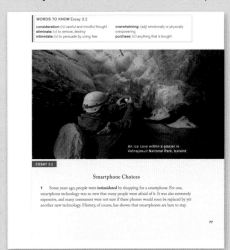

PART 3: **Building Better Sentences**
focuses students on sentence-level work to ensure more accurate writing.

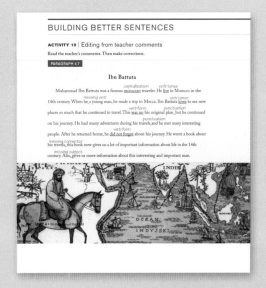

PART 4: **Writing activities** allow students to apply what they have learned by guiding them through the process of writing, editing, and revising.

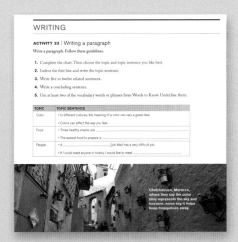

NEW Test Prep section prepares students for timed writing on high-stakes tests.

SUPPORT FOR INSTRUCTORS AND STUDENTS

FOR INSTRUCTORS

The Classroom Presentation Tool brings the classroom to life by including all Student Book pages, answers, and games to practice vocabulary.

Assessment: ExamView allows instructors to create custom tests and quizzes in minutes. **ExamView** and **Ready to Go Tests** are available online at the teacher companion website for ease of use.

FOR STUDENTS

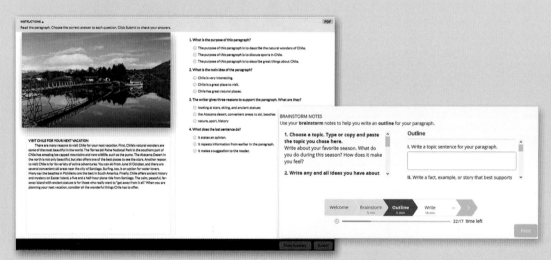

The Online Workbook provides additional practice in vocabulary, grammar, and writing, plus remediation activities for students who have not mastered at-level vocabulary and grammar.

NEW Guided online writing practice reinforces the writing process, helping students become stronger and more independent writers.

ACKNOWLEDGEMENTS

The Authors and Publisher would like to acknowledge and thank the teachers around the world who participated in the development of the fifth edition of *Great Writing*.

Asia

Anthony Brian Gallagher, Meijo University, Nagoya

Atsuko Aoki, Aoyama Gakuin University, Tokyo

Atsushi Taguchi, Okayama University of Science, Imabari Campus, Ehime

Helen Hanae, Reitaku University, Kashiwa

Hiroko Shikano, Juchi Medical University, Gotemba

Hisashi Shigematsu, Toyo Gakeun University, Tokyo

Jeremiah L. Hall, Meijo University, Nagoya

Jian Liang Fu, Kwansei Gakuin University, Nishinomiya

Jim Hwang, Yonsei University, Asan

John C. Pulaski, Chuo University and Tokyo Woman's Christian University, Tokyo

Junyawan Suwannarat, Chiang Mai University, Chiang Mai

Katherine Bauer, Clark Memorial International High School, Chiba

Kazuyo Ishibashi, Aoyama Gakuin Univeristy, Tokyo

Lei Na, Jump A-Z, Nanjing

Lor Kiat Seng, Southern University College, Seremban

Mark McClure, Kansai Gaidai Univeristy, Osaka

Matthew Shapiro, Konan Boys High School, Ashiya

Nattalak Thirachotikun, Chiang Mai University, Chiang Rai

Nick Boyes, Meijo University, Nagoya

Nick Collier, Ritsumeikan Uji Junior and Senior High School, Kobe

Olesya Shatunova, Kanagawa University, Yokohama

Pattanapichet Fasawang, Bangkok University International College, Bangkok

Paul Hansen, Hokkaido University, Sapporo

Paul Salisbury, Aichi University, Nagoya

Randall Cotten, Gifu City Women's College, Gifu

Sayaka Karlin, Toyo Gakuen University, Tokyo

Scott Gray, Clark Memorial International High School Umeda Campus, Osaka

Selina Richards, HELP University, Kuala Lumpur

Terrelle Bernard Griffin, No. 2 High School of East China Normal University-International Division, Shanghai

William Pellowe, Kinki University, Fukuoka

Yoko Hirase, Hiroshima Kokusai Gakuin University, Hiroshima

Youngmi Lim, Shinshu University, Matsumoto

Zachary Fish, RDFZ Xishan School AP Center, Beijing

USA

Amanda Kmetz, BIR Training Center, Chicago, Illinois

Amy Friedman, The American Language Institute, San Diego, California

Amy Litman, College of Southern Nevada, Las Vegas, Nevada

Angela Lehman, Virginia Commonwealth University, Richmond, Virginia

Aylin Bunk, Mount Hood Community College, Portland, Oregon

Barbara Silas, South Seattle College, Seattle, Washington

Bette Brickman, College of Southern Nevada, Las Vegas, Nevada

Breana Bayraktar, Northern Virginia Community College, Fairfax, Virginia

Carolyn Ho, Lone Star College-CyFair, Cypress, Texas

Celeste Flowers, University of Central Arkansas, Conway, Arkansas

Christina Abella, The College of Chicago, Chicago, Illinois

Christine Lines, College of Southern Nevada, Las Vegas, Nevada

Clare Roh, Howard Community College, Columbia, Maryland

DeLynn MacQueen, Columbus State Community College, Columbus, Ohio

Eleanor Molina, Northern Essex Community College, Lawrence, Massachusetts

Emily Brown, Hillsborough Community College, Florida

Emily Cakounes, North Shore Community College, Medford, Massachusetts

Erica Lederman, BIR Training Center, Chicago, Illinois

Erin Zoranski, Delaware Technical Community College, Wilmington, Delaware

Eugene Polissky, University of Potomac, Washington, DC

Farideh Hezaveh, Northern Virginia Community College, Sterling, Virginia

Gretchen Hack, Community College of Denver, Denver, Colorado

Heather Snavely, California Baptist University, Riverside, California

Hilda Tamen, University of Texas Rio Grande Valley, Edinburg, Texas

Holly Milkowart, Johnson County Community College, Overland Park, Kansas

Jessica Weimer, Cascadia College, Bothell, Washington

Jill Pagels, Lonestar Community College, Houston, Texas

Jonathan Murphy, Virginia Commonwealth University, Richmond, Virginia

Joseph Starr, Houston Community College, Southwest, Houston, Texas

Judy Chmielecki, Northern Essex Community College, Lawrence, Massachusetts

Kate Baldridge-Hale, Valencia College, Orlando, Florida

Kathleen Biache, Miami Dade College, Miami, Florida

Katie Edwards, Howard Community College, Columbia, Maryland

Kenneth Umland, College of Southern Nevada, Las Vegas, Nevada

FROM THE AUTHORS

Great Writing began in 1998 when three of us were teaching writing and frequently found ourselves complaining about the lack of materials for English language learners. A lot of books talked about writing but did not ask the students to write until the end of a chapter. In essence, the material seemed to be more of a lecture followed by "Now you write an essay." Students were reading a lot but writing little. What was missing was useful sequenced instruction for developing ESL writers by getting them to write.

Each of us had folders with our own original tried-and-true activities, so we set out to combine our materials into a coherent book that would help teachers and students alike. The result was *Great Paragraphs* and *Great Essays*, the original books of the *Great Writing* series. Much to our surprise, the books were very successful. Teachers around the world reached out to us and offered encouragement and ideas. Through the past four editions we have listened to those ideas, improved upon the books, and added four more levels.

We are proud to present this 5th edition of the *Great Writing* series with the same tried-and-true focus on writing and grammar, but with an added emphasis on developing accurate sentences and expanding level-appropriate academic vocabulary.

We thank those who have been involved in the development of this series over the years. In particular for the 5th edition, we would like to thank Laura Le Dréan, Executive Editor; the developmental editors for this edition: Lisl Bove, Eve Yu, Yeny Kim, Jennifer Monaghan, and Tom Jefferies. We will be forever grateful to two people who shaped our original books: Susan Maguire and Kathy Sands-Boehmer. Without all of these professionals, our books would most definitely not be the great works they are right now.

As always, we look forward to hearing your feedback and ideas as you use these materials with your students.

Sincerely,

Keith Folse
April Muchmore-Vokoun
Elena Vestri
David Clabeaux
Tison Pugh

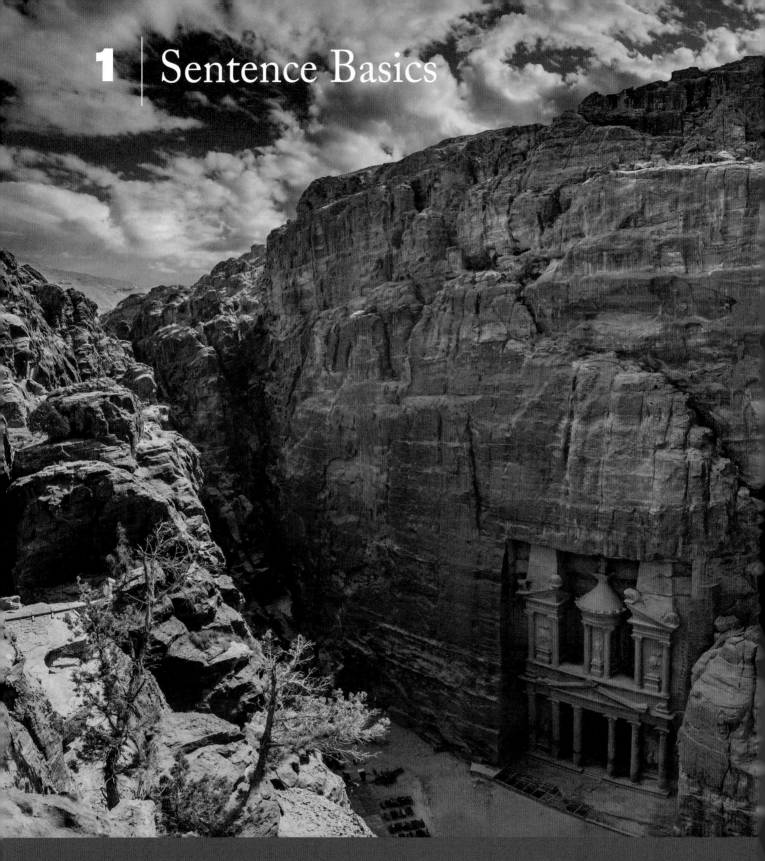

1 | Sentence Basics

OBJECTIVES
- Use common sentence patterns with the verb *be*
- Write sentences with *there is/there are*
- Use prepositional phrases of place and time
- Use time words and phrases
- Use correct capitalization and punctuation

Al-Khazneh is an ancient building in Petra, Jordan.

FREEWRITE | Look at the photo. On a separate piece of paper, write what you know or want to know about this place. Why do people build places like this?

ELEMENTS OF GREAT WRITING

What Is a Sentence?

A **simple sentence** is a group of words that:

- expresses a complete thought
- has a subject and a verb
- has an object and/or other information after the verb

SUBJECT	VERB	OBJECT	OTHER INFORMATION
Maria	sings.		
Maria and her sister	play	the piano.	
They	sing and play	beautiful songs	every day.
Maria's brother	plays	soccer and basketball.	

The **subject:**

- is the person or thing that does the action
- can be a noun or a pronoun

The **verb:**

- shows the action or state of the subject
- is sometimes an action word, such as *go, speak, write, swim,* or *watch*
- is sometimes a non-action word, such as *be, like, want,* or *need*

The **object:**

- receives the action of the verb
- can be a noun or a pronoun

ACTIVITY 1 | Identifying subjects, verbs, and objects

Underline the subject in each sentence. Circle the verb(s). Double underline any objects.

1. My friend and I play tennis.

2. Eun and Hae-Won skate.

3. The university has business and education classes.

4. Abdullah and Salem take and share pictures.

5. The science class studies climate change.

6. The history professors give long lectures.

7. Eva reads newspapers, magazines, and books.

8. The performer sings, acts, and dances.

ACTIVITY 2 | Using subjects, verbs, and objects

Fill in each blank with the correct subject, verb, or object. Use words from the word box.

Amazon Go	Caroline	enjoys	She	wakes up
arrives	classes	her job	takes	works

> **WORDS TO KNOW** Paragraph 1.1
>
> **attend:** (v) to go to a meeting, class, and so on   **break:** (n) a pause or stop in work or activity

PARAGRAPH 1.1

A Great Place to Work

¹_____ has a great job at Amazon Go. ²_____ works there on Mondays, Tuesdays, and Thursdays. She does not work there on Wednesdays because she **attends** ³_____ at Jefferson Community College. On her workdays, Caroline ⁴_____ at 6 a.m. She ⁵_____ at the store at 8 a.m. She ⁶_____ from 8 a.m. to 5 p.m. She ⁷_____ her **break** from 12:30 p.m. to 1:30 p.m. Caroline likes ⁸_____ very much. She ⁹_____ her coworkers, too. For Caroline, ¹⁰_____ is a great place to work.

An Amazon Go customer uses an app to buy groceries.

5

Avoiding Fragments

A **fragment** is an incomplete sentence. It:

- is missing a subject or a verb
- does not have a complete idea

    ✓ John is my brother. **He** works at Ames Bank.

    ✗ John is my brother. Works at Ames Bank.

    ✓ Many people **have** white cars.

    ✗ Many people white cars.

Check your work to avoid writing fragments.

<table>
<tr><td>

WRITER'S NOTE Using *It* as a Subject

Use *It* as the subject to talk about weather and time. Without the *It* subject, you have a fragment.

    ✓ **It** snows a lot this time of year.

    ✗ Snows a lot this time of year.

    ✓ **It** is five o'clock now.

    ✗ Is five o'clock now.

</td></tr>
</table>

ACTIVITY 3 | Identifying fragments

Write F for *fragment* and S for *complete sentence*. Then correct the fragments.

1. ___S___ Hans lives in a big apartment.

2. ___F___ My mother ⌃makes breakfast every morning.

3. _____ Is sunny today.

4. _____ Abdul has a car.

5. _____ They my cousins from Miami.

6. _____ It twelve o'clock.

7. _____ Michael likes football.

8. _____ Nicole and Jean best friends.

9. _____ Colombia is in South America.

10. _____ Has a subject and a verb.

Sentences with the Verb *Be*

Be is a very common verb in English. It has three forms in the simple present: *am, is, are.*
Be is never followed by an object. Here are three common sentence patterns of *be.*

Subject + *Be* + Adjective(s)

SUBJECT	BE	ADJECTIVE(S)
I	am	happy.
You/We/They	are	young.
He/She/It	is	fun and interesting.

Subject + *Be* + Noun(s)/Noun Phrase

SUBJECT	BE	NOUN(S)/NOUN PHRASE
I	am	a mother and a doctor.
The players	are	a team.
Ceviche	is	a seafood dish.

Subject + *Be* + Prepositional Phrase

SUBJECT	BE	PREPOSITIONAL PHRASE
I	am	at school.
My keys	are	on the table.
The test	is	in the morning.

You can use more than one pattern at a time in a sentence:

            adj   prep phr
I **am** happy at work.

             n phr   prep phr
She **is** a top chef in Asia.

Chef Chen Lansu at her
restaurant, Le Moût, in Taiwan

ACTIVITY 4 | Identifying sentence patterns of *be*

Read the paragraph. Then follow the directions below.

1. Circle the sentence(s) with the pattern *be* + adjective(s).
2. Underline the sentence(s) with the pattern *be* + noun(s)/noun phrase.
3. Double underline the sentence(s) with the pattern *be* + prepositional phrase.

> **WORDS TO KNOW** Paragraph 1.2
>
> **border:** (n) the line that divides two countries   **scientist:** (n) someone who works in science
> **research:** (n) the study of information

PARAGRAPH 1.2

A Language Scientist

Sandhya Narayanan is a National Geographic Explorer. She is from Boston, USA, and Toronto, Canada. She speaks many languages. She is a language **scientist**. Sandhya works in the Andes Mountains on the **border** of Peru and Bolivia. She studies two languages there. These languages are old. They are Quechua and Aymara. She studies the change of these languages over time. Her **research** teaches us about languages in the world.

Sandhya Narayanan

ACTIVITY 5 | Scrambled sentences

Unscramble the words and phrases to write complete sentences.

1. My name / Angela / is

My name is Angela_____.

2. from Kearney, Nebraska / I / am

_____.

3. in the middle of the United States / a small city / Kearney / is

_____.

4. a professor / My mother / is

_____.

5. My father / a small business owner / is

_____.

6. am / the oldest child / I / in my family

_____.

7. tall / I / am

_____.

8. Hiking / is / my hobby

_____.

9. am / I / an / English teacher

_____.

10. is / Teaching / exciting and fun

_____.

ACTIVITY 6 | Writing sentences

A. Write eight simple sentences about yourself. Follow the examples in Activity 5.

1. _____

2. _____

3. _____

4. _____

5. _____

6. _____

7. _____

8. _____

B. Take turns reading your sentences to a partner. Then write three or four things you learned about him/her.

1. _____

2. _____

3. _____

4. _____

Grammar: Expressing Place and Time

A **prepositional phrase** is a group of words that:

- begins with a preposition, such as *at, in,* or *on*
- includes a noun or pronoun, called the object of the preposition

A **prepositional phrase of place** tells about location. It answers the question *Where?* We usually put it at the end of a sentence.

> We eat a lot of salad **at home**.
>
> The computer is **on the desk**.
>
> Loretta lives **in my house**.

A **prepositional phrase of time** tells about time. It answers the question *When?* We usually put it at the end of a sentence. It often goes after a prepositional phrase of place if both are present.

> Michelle reads the newspaper **in the morning**.
>
> She sees him <u>at the bank</u> **on Mondays**.

A **time word** or **time phrase** also answers the question *When?* and can come at the end of a sentence.

> Eric watches TV **daily**.
>
> Marco works **every afternoon**.

If you start a sentence with an expression of time, it is common to use a comma.

> **In the spring,** everyone has finals.
>
> **Today,** we have an important meeting.
>
> **Twice a week,** Teresa volunteers at the library.

Here are some common ways to express place and time.

PREPOSITIONAL PHRASES OF PLACE	PREPOSITIONAL PHRASES OF TIME	TIME WORDS AND PHRASES
at school	at 9:00 a.m.	today
at the bank	at noon	now
on the wall	at night	every day
on Main Street	in the morning	once a week
in the bag	on Saturdays	twice a month
in Istanbul	on October 14	three times a year

For more information on the prepositions *at*, *in*, and *on*, see the *Writer's Handbook*.

ACTIVITY 7 | Scrambled sentences

Unscramble the words and phrases to write complete sentences.

1. Amal / five days a week / works / at the hospital

   _____.

2. Silvia and Ana / twice a week / at City College / grammar / study

   _____.

3. at the gym / exercises / Janie / every day

   _____.

4. we / take / every week / in Mrs. Wang's class / an important quiz

   _____.

5. puts / Eric / his books / in the afternoon / in his car

   _____.

6. eats dinner / once a week / Sulaiman / at a restaurant

   _____.

7. Sara / once a month / a pie / bakes / in the oven

   _____.

8. I / busy / right now / am / at work

   _____.

9. Paul and Carrie / their grandmother / every month / visit / in Miami

   _____.

10. we / coffee / have / every morning / at the café

   _____.

Grammar: *There Is/There Are* + Prepositional Phrase

Use *there is/there are* to say that something exists. Use **there is/there are + a prepositional phrase** to say where something is. When you begin a sentence with *there*, the subject follows the verb *be*. Use *is* with singular subjects. Use *are* with plural subjects.

THERE	IS/ARE	SUBJECT	PREPOSITIONAL PHRASE
There	is	one Earth.	
There	is	a meeting	in the conference room.
There	are	two types of elephants.	
There	are	two empty chairs	at the table.

ACTIVITY 8 | Analyzing a paragraph

Read the paragraph. Underline the five sentences with *there is* and *there are*. Number them 1-5. Then answer the questions that follow.

> **WORDS TO KNOW** Paragraph 1.3
>
> **common:** (adj) usual
> **leader:** (n) a person in control of a situation or place
> **location:** (n) place
>
> **object:** (n) thing
> **simple:** (adj) basic, uncomplicated

A classroom in Oman

PARAGRAPH 1.3

My Colorful Classroom

My classroom is very colorful. There are twenty desks [1] in the room. Each desk has a dark brown seat and a shiny white top. There is a world map on the left side of the room. This map shows the **locations** of all the countries in the world, and each continent[1] is a different color. There are two posters on the right side of the room. There is a list of fifty **common** verbs on the first poster. The second poster has some **simple** pictures of fruits and vegetables. On the bulletin board, there are some pictures of famous **leaders**. These **objects** make my classroom colorful.

[1]continent: one of the seven main areas of land on the Earth (Africa, Antarctica, Asia, Australia, Europe, North America, and South America)

1. Which sentences use *there are*? _____

2. What are the subjects of these sentences? _____
   _____

3. Which sentences use *there is*? _____

4. What are the subjects of these sentences? _____
   _____

5. Where is the world map? _____

6. Where are the posters? _____

7. Where are the pictures of famous leaders? _____

ACTIVITY 9 | Editing a paragraph

The paragraph has four errors with *there is/there are*. Find and correct them.

> **WORDS TO KNOW** Paragraph 1.4
>
> **follow:** (v) to go after

PARAGRAPH 1.4

The English Alphabet

There have 26 letters in the English alphabet. There is five vowel letters and 21 consonant letters. The five vowels are *a, e, i, o,* and *u.* The letters *w* and *y* can be vowels when they **follow** other vowels. There three letters with the *a* sound in their names. These letters are *a, j,* and *k.* Are nine letters with the *e* sound in their names. These are *b, c, d, e, g, p, t, v,* and *z.* If you want to write well in English, you must learn the 26 letters of the English alphabet.

The Nomade sculpture in Antibes, France, is made of steel letters.

ACTIVITY 10 | Using *there is/there are* + prepositional phrase

Choose *is* or *are* to complete the first part of the sentence. Then fill in the blank with the correct prepositional phrase of place.

at the beach	at the zoo	in the park	on the table
at the library	in a rainbow	in the parking lot	on the test
at the museum	in the class	on the bus	on TV

1. There (is / are) seven colors _____.

2. There (is / are) many types of art _____.

3. There (is / are) students from different countries _____.

4. There (is / are) a beautiful garden _____.

5. There (is / are) many different animals _____.

6. There (is / are) a dirty plate _____.

7. There (is / are) so many cars _____.

8. There (is / are) a new reading room _____.

9. There (is / are) difficult questions _____.

10. There (is / are) a funny show _____.

11. There (is / are) a passenger _____.

12. There (is / are) people swimming _____.

ACTIVITY 11 | Analyzing a paragraph

Read the paragraph. Underline the subject and circle the verb in each sentence. Double underline any objects. Then answer the questions that follow.

> **WORDS TO KNOW** Paragraph 1.5
>
> **cover:** (v) to hide something by putting another thing over it
> **main:** (adj) most important
>
> **middle:** (n) the central part of something
> **practice:** (n) repeated activity to help you become better at something

Students at Inuyama Junior High School in Japan take part in the tradition of washing their desks and chairs in the Kisogawa River.

PARAGRAPH 1.5

A Student's Desk

¹There are four school books in the **middle** of my desk. ²The two large books **cover** the desk. ³They are textbooks. ⁴One is a grammar book. ⁵It is green. ⁶There is a writing book next to the grammar book. ⁷It is blue. ⁸The other books are smaller. ⁹They are on top of the textbooks. ¹⁰They are workbooks. ¹¹The textbooks have the **main** information. ¹²The workbooks have more **practice**. ¹³These four books are always on my desk.

1. What is the noun phrase in sentence 4? _____

2. What is the prepositional phrase of place in sentence 9? _____

3. Which sentences have objects? _____

4. Which sentences follow the pattern *be* + adjective? _____

ACTIVITY 12 | Writing sentences

Write ten simple sentences about the picture. Make sure that every sentence has a subject and a verb. Write at least one sentence with each of the following: *there is, there are, be* + adjective, and *be* + prepositional phrase of place.

1. The couch and chair are yellow.

2. _____

3. _____

4. _____

5. _____

6. _____

7. _____

8. _____

9. _____

10. _____

Mechanics: Beginning and Ending a Sentence

In English, there are two kinds of letters: **capital** and **lowercase**.

Capital Letters	A B C D E F G H I J K L M N O P Q R S T U V W X Y Z
Lowercase Letters	a b c d e f g h i j k l m n o p q r s t u v w x y z

We always begin a sentence with a capital letter.

✓ The boxes on the table are heavy.

✗ the boxes on the table are heavy.

A period (.) is the most common way to end a sentence.

✓ Brazil is a large country.

✗ Brazil is a large country

ACTIVITY 13 | Scrambled sentences

Unscramble the words and phrases to write complete sentences. Use correct capitalization and punctuation.

1. love / children around the world / soccer / to play

_____

2. do not / children in some countries / money / have / for a ball

_____

3. are / these children / very clever

_____

4. their own / make / soccer balls / they

_____

5. start with / they / old shopping bags and paper

_____

6. they / around the materials / wrap / string

_____

7. makes / a strong ball / this / to play with

_____

8. are / the children / happy / to play with / these hand-made soccer balls

_____

Mechanics: Using Capital Letters with Proper Nouns

A **proper noun** is a specific person, place, or thing, and always begins with a capital letter.

PROPER NOUN	EXAMPLES
The Name of a Person	One famous person in history is **N**elson **M**andela. **T**oni **M**orrison is an award-winning author.
The Name of a Place	My favorite city is **N**ew **Y**ork **C**ity. The capital of **Q**atar is **D**oha.
The Title of Something	Paco loves the movie ***Star Wars: The Last Jedi***. Our class is reading ***Great Expectations***.
Days and Months	The first **S**unday of **J**uly is an important day to me. The fourth **T**hursday in **N**ovember is a holiday in the United States.
Languages and Countries	In **I**ndia, the most common languages are **H**indi and **E**nglish. The official languages of **C**anada are **E**nglish and **F**rench.

For a complete list of capitalization rules, see the *Writer's Handbook*.

ACTIVITY 14 | Editing a paragraph

Correct the capitalization mistake(s) in each sentence.

> **WORDS TO KNOW** Paragraph 1.6
>
> **own:** (v) to have something that is yours
> **popular:** (adj) liked by many people
> **reliable:** (adj) able to be trusted
>
> **tourist:** (n) someone traveling or visiting a place for fun
> **variety:** (n) different types of things

PARAGRAPH 1.6

An Interesting Job

¹ M
my cousin albert has an interesting job. ²he is a taxi driver in chicago. ³albert **owns** his own taxi company. ⁴it is called **reliable** taxi service. ⁵albert drives a taxi every day except sunday. ⁶may and june are busy months for him. ⁷**tourists** from canada and europe often use albert's company. ⁸he drives his passengers to a **variety** of locations. ⁹**popular** places are the john hancock observatory, millennium park, and wrigley field. ¹⁰ my cousin practices english with his customers. ¹¹albert loves his job.

BUILDING BETTER VOCABULARY

ACTIVITY 15 | Word associations

Circle the word or phrase that is more closely related to the bold word on the left.

1. attend	leave something	go to something
2. break	brief stop	quick start
3. common	unusual	usual
4. follow	go after	go before
5. main	different	important
6. middle	center	edge
7. own	have	sell
8. popular	hated	liked
9. simple	difficult	easy
10. variety	one	several

ACTIVITY 16 | Collocations

Fill in the blank with the word that most naturally completes the phrase.

attend	break	common	communicate	leader

1. _____ clearly

2. a group _____

3. take a _____

4. _____ an English class

5. make a _____ mistake

| location | middle | reliable | research | tourist |

6. a _____ attraction

7. a _____ source of information

8. more _____ is necessary

9. in the _____ of a project

10. a central _____

ACTIVITY 17 | Word forms

Complete each sentence with the correct word form. Use the correct form of the nouns and verbs.

NOUN	VERB	ADJECTIVE	SENTENCE
attendance	attend		**1.** Mr. Cox checks the students' _____ every day. **2.** Do you _____ any classes in the evenings?
cover	cover	covered	**3.** I have a _____ on my smart phone. **4.** Amal _____ her head with a scarf every day.
practice	practice		**5.** Do you have soccer _____ today? **6.** Eva _____ her English at the language club.
scientist		scientific	**7.** The _____ magazine publishes all the latest research. **8.** Neil deGrasse Tyson is a _____ and a TV host.
variety	vary	various	**9.** There are _____ ways to study vocabulary. **10.** This menu has a _____ of vegetarian foods.

ACTIVITY 18 | Vocabulary in writing

Choose five words from Words to Know. Write a complete sentence with each word.

1. _____

2. _____

3. _____

4. _____

5. _____

BUILDING BETTER SENTENCES

ACTIVITY 19 | Editing sentences

Find and correct the errors. The number in parentheses tells how many errors each sentence has.

1. Gyeongju National park is in south Korea (3)

2. Most schools classes in may. (2)

3. My family at the pool swims. (1)

4. In the winter, snows a lot in the mountains (2)

5. Jane classes at Houston Community College. (1)

6. There is on the table a big dinner. (1)

7. mr. Smith the most popular teacher this semester in our school. (3)

8. The pacific ocean is the largest ocean in the world. (2)

9. The official language of china is mandarin (3)

10. You can find in a Museum many beautiful types of art. (2)

ACTIVITY 20 | Editing sentences

Some of the sentences have errors with missing subjects, missing verbs, punctuation, or capitalization. Check (√) whether each sentence is correct or incorrect. Correct the incorrect sentences.

	Correct	Incorrect
1. Mexico ^is^ not near Great Britain.	☐	☑
2. The Bahla Fort is in ~~o~~man. (O)	☐	☑
3. Sudan is in Africa	☐	☐
4. Portland is a popular city in Oregon, USA.	☐	☐
5. Austria and Hungary are in Europe.	☐	☐
6. Russia and Canada bigger than the United States.	☐	☐
7. Rains a lot in Southeast Asia during the rainy season.	☐	☐
8. Three main groups of people live in Malaysia.	☐	☐
9. Nepal is north of India.	☐	☐
10. Bolivia not part of Europe.	☐	☐

Combining Sentences

Some writers like to keep their sentences short because they feel that if they write longer and more complicated sentences, they are more likely to make mistakes. However, longer sentences connect ideas, and this makes it easier for the reader to understand.

Study these sentences. The important information is circled.

I (have) a (friend,)

My friend (studies science.)

My friend studies (at the university.)

Every sentence has an important piece of information. The most important information from each sentence can be used to create longer and smoother sentences. Notice how the ideas in the shorter sentences are combined in these longer sentences.

My friend is a science student at the university.

I have a friend who studies science at the university.

A word or word form may change or be omitted, but no ideas are changed or omitted. Remember that there is usually more than one way to combine sentences.

Study these sentences. The important information is circled.

There was a (storm) (yesterday.)

It was (strong.)

It (moved) (quickly) (toward the city.)

Now read these longer, smoother sentences:

Yesterday, a strong storm moved quickly toward the city.

There was a strong storm that moved quickly toward the city yesterday.

ACTIVITY 21 | Combining sentences

Combine the ideas into one sentence. You may change the word forms, but do not change or omit any ideas. There may be more than one answer.

1. Andrew is a teacher.
   Andrew is reliable.
   Andrew teaches at my high school.

   _____

2. There are answers.
   The answers are correct.
   The answers are on the website.

   _____

3. Rachel takes Tai Chi classes.
   The classes are at a park.
   The park is popular.

   _____

Students do Tai Chi in Chongqing, China.

WRITING

ACTIVITY 22 | Writing sentences

Write original sentences. Follow the instructions.

- Answer the questions below to write eight to ten complete sentences about a famous location (city, country, or area) you want to visit.
- As you write, use at least two vocabulary words or phrases presented in this unit. Underline these words in your sentences.

1. What famous location do you want to visit? _____

_____

2. Where is this location? _____

_____

3. What is an important monument or place there? _____

_____

4. Briefly describe this monument or place. _____

_____

_____

5. What is another thing this location is known for? _____

_____

6. Briefly explain. _____

_____

7. What is an interesting thing to see or do in this location? _____

_____

8. Briefly explain. _____

_____

Editing

It is a good idea to check your work for grammar, spelling, and punctuation. You should also make sure your writing is clear and easy to understand.

After you finish writing, check your work for errors. Use the checklist below to help you.

- ☐ Each sentence has a subject and a verb.
- ☐ Each sentence starts with a capital letter and ends with a period.
- ☐ I used the verb *be* correctly.
- ☐ I used *there are* with plural subjects and *there is* with singular subjects.
- ☐ I used prepositional phrases of place correctly.
- ☐ I capitalized all proper nouns.
- ☐ I used vocabulary words from the unit correctly.

Peer Editing

A good way to make sure that your writing is clear is to let someone else read it and make suggestions. Other people may notice things that you missed.

After you check your work, it is helpful to have a peer check it. A peer is someone who is equal to you, such as a classmate. When a peer edits your writing, it is called peer editing.

This is what usually happens in peer editing:

1. A peer reads your writing.

2. Your peer gives you suggestions and ideas for making your writing better.

3. You listen carefully to what your peer says.

4. You think about making the changes your peer suggests. If the comments are negative, remember that the comments are about the mistakes in your writing, not about you.

Peer Editing Comments

When you peer edit a classmate's writing, choose your words carefully. Make sure that:

- Your comments are helpful. Be specific about the mistakes.

  Helpful: "You forgot to put the word *at* here."
  Not helpful: "This is incorrect."

- Your comments are polite. Say things the way you would want someone to tell you.

  Polite: "What does this sentence mean? Can you make the meaning clearer?"
  Not polite: "What is this? It doesn't make any sense at all!"

Before you write a comment, ask yourself, "Will this be helpful to the writer? Would I want someone to tell me this?"

ACTIVITY 23 | Writing peer editing comments

Edit the paragraph. There are mistakes with capitalization, punctuation, and fragments. Then complete the feedback below. Compare your comments with a partner.

Sunset in Siena, Italy

PARAGRAPH 1.7

The Beauty of Tuscany

I want to visit tuscany. Tuscany _T a beautiful location in Italy. The apennine

Mountains in Tuscany. Have great places to ski and hike. Tuscany also famous for its

beautiful ceramics[1]. For example, bowls, vases, and oil jars very popular with tourists.

Tuscany has so many interesting places to see. Pisa and Siena two beautiful cities there.

Is a wonderful place to visit

[1]ceramics: pottery; items made of oven-dried clay

1. Write one positive comment about the paragraph.

_____

2. Write one thing the writer can improve when he or she rewrites the paragraph.

_____

ACTIVITY 24 | Peer editing

Exchange books with a partner and look at Activity 22. Read your partner's sentences. Then use Peer Editing Form 1 in the *Writer's Handbook* to comment on your partner's sentences. Offer positive suggestions and comments that will help your partner improve his or her writing. Consider your partner's comments as you revise your own sentences.

Additional Topics for Writing

Choose one or more of the topics to write about. Follow your teacher's directions.

TOPIC 1: Look back at the photo and caption on pages 2–3. Describe an amazing location in your country. Where is it? What is it? Why is it amazing?

TOPIC 2: Describe an interesting job someone you know has. What things does this person have to do for that job?

TOPIC 3: Write about your favorite type of animal. Why do you like this animal? Where does this animal normally live? What does the animal look like?

TOPIC 4: Write about your weekends. What do you like to do? Who do you spend your weekends with?

TOPIC 5: Write about a hobby that you have. What is it? How often do you do it? Why do you enjoy this hobby?

TEST PREP

You should spend about 25 minutes on this task. Write a paragraph with six to ten sentences.

Some people prefer to spend their free time indoors. Other people prefer to spend their free time outdoors. Which do you prefer? Give specific reasons and examples.

> **TIP**
> Take five to seven minutes to think of ideas before you begin writing. Take notes on these ideas. This will help you write your response more quickly and clearly.

Remember to use complete sentences. Check your work for fragments and correct capitalization and punctuation.

2 | Paragraph Basics

OBJECTIVES
- Identify topic, supporting, and concluding sentences
- Use adjectives
- Use subject and object pronouns
- Write an original paragraph

Nobel Prize-winning author Gabriel Garcia Marquez greets people from a train window in his hometown of Aracataca, Colombia.

FREEWRITE | Look at the photo and read the caption. What is happening? Why?

ELEMENTS OF GREAT WRITING

What Is a Paragraph?

A **paragraph** is a group of sentences about one topic or idea. It has four main parts:

- an indented (moved in) first line
- a topic sentence that gives the main idea
- a body of sentences all about the main idea
- a concluding sentence

ACTIVITY 1 | Analyzing paragraphs

Read the paragraphs and answer the questions that follow.

> **WORDS TO KNOW** Paragraphs 2.1 to 2.2
>
> **amazing:** (adj) causing great surprise or wonder
> **bother:** (v) to annoy someone
>
> **comfortable:** (adj) providing relaxation
> **relax:** (v) to stop work and enjoy oneself

PARAGRAPH 2.1

The Best Place to Relax

My back porch is my favorite place to **relax**. First, it has a lot of **comfortable** chairs with soft pillows. I feel so good when I sit in them. My back porch is also very quiet. I can sit and think there. I can even read a great book and nobody **bothers** me. Finally, in the evening, I can sit on my porch and watch the sunset. Watching the beautiful colors always calms me. I can relax in many places, but my back porch is the best.

A colorful porch in New York, USA

1. The topic sentence is the first sentence. Write it here.

_____

2. What is the main idea of this paragraph?

   a. The writer likes watching the sunset.

   b. The writer likes to read a book in a quiet place.

   c. The writer likes to relax on her back porch.

3. Write the four things the writer does to relax on her porch.

a. _She sits in comfortable chairs._

b. _____

c. _____

d. _____

4. How many sentences are in this paragraph? _____

5. The concluding sentence is the last sentence. Write it here.

_____

PARAGRAPH 2.2

The Shanghai Tower

The Shanghai Tower in China is an **amazing** building. It is the tallest building in Shanghai's business district[1], and the second-tallest building in the world. The tower has 128 floors, and there are more levels below the building. It has 107 elevators, and they can move 40 mph. There are beautiful gardens on many floors, and the Shanghai Tower has one of the world's highest observation decks[2]. In addition, the tower is good for the environment. Special machines use the wind to make extra electricity for the building, and the building uses rainwater to keep it cool inside. The Shanghai Tower is amazing inside and out.

[1]district: an area of a city or a country
[2]observation deck: the top of a building where people can look at everything below

The Shanghai Tower rises above the Shanghai World Financial Center and the Jin Mao Tower.

1. What is the topic sentence? Write it here.

_____

2. What is the main idea of this paragraph?

    a. The Shanghai Tower is good for the environment.

    b. The Shanghai Tower is tall.

    c. The Shanghai Tower is wonderful.

3. Write six amazing things about the Shanghai Tower.

    a. _____

    b. _____

    c. _____

    d. _____

    e. _____

    f. _____

4. How many sentences are in this paragraph? _____

5. What is the concluding sentence? Write it here.

_____

Mechanics: The Title of a Paragraph

A **title** gives the reader information about what is in a paragraph. A good title:

- tells the main topic, but does not tell about everything in the paragraph
- is usually short—sometimes only one word
- does not have a period at the end
- does not begin with _My Paragraph_
- follows special capitalization rules

The capitalization rules for titles are:

- always capitalize the first letter of the first word
- only capitalize the first letter of the important words in the rest of the title
- do not capitalize a preposition or an article unless it is the first word

    How to Take a Good Picture with a Cell Phone

    An Amazing Vacation

ACTIVITY 2 | Editing titles

With a partner discuss what is wrong with each title. Then edit each one to make it a good title.

1. AN INFLUENTIAL INVENTOR

2. A Handbook For International Students In Canada

3. Three Types of Transportation.

4. My Paragraph on a New Technology

5. How to Become an Engineer at NASA in a Very Short Amount of Time

6. The ten Best Movies of All Time

7. This Was the Best Day of My Life.

8. My first car

9. an Unusual Animal

10. the first female astronaut

ACTIVITY 3 | Writing a paragraph

Answer the questions. Use complete sentences.

1. Who is a popular person in your country?

   _____

2. Where is this person from?

   _____

3. What does this person do?

   _____

4. Why is this person popular?

   _____

5. Do you like this person? Why or why not?

   _____

Now write your sentences in paragraph form on a separate piece of paper. Remember to indent the first line and give your paragraph a title.

Parts of a Paragraph: The Topic Sentence

A good paragraph has a **topic sentence**. The topic sentence:

- tells the main idea of the whole paragraph
- is often the first sentence
- should not be too specific or too general

If a paragraph does not have a topic sentence, the reader may be confused because the organization of ideas will not be clear.

ACTIVITY 4 | Identifying topic sentences

Paragraphs 2.3, 2.4, and 2.5 are each missing a topic sentence. Read each paragraph. Then choose the best topic sentence.

WORDS TO KNOW Paragraphs 2.3 to 2.5

accident: (n) a harmful or unpleasant event that happens by surprise
compete: (v) to participate in a contest
damage: (v) to hurt or injure
danger: (n) a harmful situation
during: (prep) all through a time period
energy: (n) activity

explore: (v) to travel around to learn more; to investigate
extremely: (adv) very
fan: (n) a person who likes something very much
traffic: (n) the movement of cars, trucks, and so on in an area

---

PARAGRAPH 2.3

Heavy snow stops traffic in Japan.

The Problems with Snow

Snow is beautiful when it falls. However, the snow is not beautiful for very long. When it starts to melt[1], the clean streets become wet and difficult to walk on. The sidewalks are slippery[2]. Snow also causes **traffic** problems. Some roads are closed. Other roads are difficult to drive on safely. Drivers have more **accidents** on snowy roads. There are more problems with snow than reasons to like it.

[1]melt: to change from a solid to a liquid
[2]slippery: causing people or things to fall or slide

a. In December, it usually snows.

b. Snow does not cause many problems.

c. Snow is beautiful, but it causes many problems.

My Favorite City

I love to see all the interesting landmarks[1] there. I always visit the Statue of Liberty and the Empire State Building. It is also fun to **explore** different areas of the city. My favorites are Chinatown and Manhattan. Most importantly, New York City is full of **energy**. People from all over the world walk on its streets, play in its parks, and eat its wonderful food. I never feel bored or alone when I am there. I truly[2] love New York City.

[1]landmark: a historic building or other point of interest
[2]truly: really; sincerely

a. My favorite city is New York City.
b. New York City is a very busy city.
c. New York City is also full of energy.

Road Cycling

Cyclists on the cycling Tour of Oman

In road cycling, cyclists **compete** on public[1] roads. These roads are usually good, but rain can make them very slippery. Serious accidents are common **during** this weather. Cyclists also ride very close together. If a rider falls, many of the others around him also fall. These accidents can **damage** bikes and hurt the riders. Finally, the cyclists are also in **danger** from their **fans.** Spectators[2] stand along the roads as the bikes speed[3] past. Fans often run next to the riders or try to touch them, and this can cause terrible problems. Road cycling may look like a safe sport, but it can be **extremely** dangerous.

[1]public: meant for use by the people in the community
[2]spectator: someone who watches an event
[3]speed: to move quickly

a. Road cycling can be a dangerous sport.
b. Road cycling fans can be a danger to bike riders.
c. Road cycling is an extremely exciting sport.

ACTIVITY 5 | Writing topic sentences

Read the paragraphs and write a topic sentence for each one. Remember to indent. Then read the paragraphs again. Make sure that each topic sentence gives the main idea for the whole paragraph.

WORDS TO KNOW Paragraphs 2.6 to 2.8

check: (v) to look for information
connect: (v) to reach by phone or Internet
explain: (v) to give information about; make clear
organized: (adj) in good order

patient: (adj) calm; not easily upset
plan: (v) to prepare for something
taste: (v) to sense the flavor of food and liquids

PARAGRAPH 2.6

Pasta, Pasta, Pasta

First, pasta **tastes** great. Sometimes I eat it plain[1]. However, I also like it with butter or cheese. Another reason I like pasta is the variety. There are many types of pasta, but my favorites are spaghetti, macaroni, vermicelli, and lasagna. In addition, pasta is very easy to prepare. I can make pasta in less than 10 minutes. Finally, pasta is a very healthy food for me. A plate of pasta has about 300 calories[2], but it has only three grams of fat. I love to eat pasta every day.

[1]plain: simple; with nothing added
[2]calorie: a measure of energy produced by food

PARAGRAPH 2.7

Why I Love My Tablet[1]

First, it **connects** me to my school and class. I **check** my class website for daily assignments and videos. In addition, I put all the due dates[2] for tests and homework into the tablet's calendar so that I am always ready for class. All my textbooks are also on it. I do not need to carry many heavy textbooks anymore. Finally, I use the tablet to complete all my writing assignments. When I finish them, I just email my work to my teacher. I never go to school without my tablet.

[1]tablet: a portable computer controlled by touch
[2]due date: the day something must be completed

A math teacher in Afghanistan

Good Teachers

First, good teachers are **patient**. They **explain** things again and again. In addition, they are **organized**. They **plan** for every class. Good teachers are also encouraging[1]. They help students understand the subject. Finally, good teachers are fair[2]. They do not give too much or too little work, and they grade students on how good their work is. These are some important qualities[3] of good teachers.

[1]encouraging: giving strength or hope
[2]fair: just; reasonable
[3]quality: something typical of someone's character and personality

Parts of a Paragraph: Supporting Sentences

Every paragraph must have sentences that support the topic sentence. These sentences make up **the body** of the paragraph and are called **supporting sentences**. They:

- give more information about the topic, such as details, examples, or reasons
- should not include ideas that are unrelated or unconnected to the topic

Read the paragraph below. The two underlined sentences are unrelated to the topic.

Making Chili

Chili is an easy dish to prepare. To make chili, cut up one large onion. Then fry it in a little vegetable oil. Next, add fresh garlic and some chili peppers. When the onions are soft, add one pound of ground meat. Stir until the meat is cooked. Sprinkle one tablespoon of red chili powder on top. <u>There are many types of chili powder.</u> After that, add four cups of diced tomatoes, one cup of water, and one can of red beans. Cover the pot and cook over low heat for about one hour. <u>Fried chicken also takes about an hour to prepare.</u> This simple recipe creates a delicious dinner.

Underline the topic sentence and cross out the two unrelated sentences in each paragraph.

PARAGRAPH 2.9

My Office

My office has everything I need to do my work. On the left side of the room, there is a large desk. My computer sits on top of the desk, and the printer sits under it. I keep important documents in its drawers. On the right side of the room, there are two beautiful bookcases. They are full of books, magazines, and computer software. My father makes bookcases and other wood furniture. A telephone and a fax machine are on a small table next to my closet. I have trouble remembering my fax number. All my office supplies are in the closet. I enjoy my office very much.

PARAGRAPH 2.10

An Energetic Neighbor

My 96-year-old neighbor, Mrs. Wills, lives alone and takes care of herself. My grandmother lived to be 87. Mrs. Wills goes to the grocery store by herself, and she does all her own cooking. She does not like to eat white rice. Mrs. Wills also cleans her own house. She puts her heavy garbage can by the street for trash collection every week. She exercises by walking on the beach. I hope to have that much energy when I am 96 years old.

A Yupik elder woman harvests grass for baskets in Alaska, USA.

Changing Celsius to Fahrenheit

Changing temperatures from Celsius to Fahrenheit is not difficult. First, multiply the Celsius temperature by 9. Then divide this answer by 5. When you finish, add 32 to your answer. The result is the temperature in Fahrenheit. Most countries report temperatures in Celsius, but the United States reports them in Fahrenheit. For example, if the Celsius temperature is 20, you multiply 20 by 9. Then you divide the answer, 180, by 5. The result is 36. If you get a different number, check your math mistake. Next, add 32, and you have the correct Fahrenheit temperature, 68. Now you can easily change a temperature from Celsius to Fahrenheit.

Grammar: Adjective + Noun

When you write, you can make a sentence much more interesting if you add descriptive words. These descriptive words are called **adjectives**. They describe nouns (people, places, things, and ideas).

	ADJECTIVE(S)	NOUN
I have a	**heavy**	bag.
This is my	**new**	bicycle.
Michael goes to an	**excellent**	college.
Rachel draws	**small ink**	pictures.

Sometimes you can combine two short sentences by putting the adjective(s) before the noun.

TWO SHORT SENTENCES	BETTER WRITING
n adj There is a <u>volcano</u>. It is **huge**.	adj n There is a **huge** <u>volcano</u>.
n adj Susan is an <u>athlete</u>. She is **talented**.	adj n Susan is a **talented** <u>athlete</u>.
adj n adj Sami drives an **old** <u>car</u>. It is **silver**.	adj adj n Sami drives an **old silver** <u>car</u>.
adj n Lisa collects **small** <u>photographs</u>. These n adj <u>photographs</u> are **antique**.	adj adj n Lisa collects **small antique** <u>photographs</u>.

For more information about order of adjectives, see the *Writer's Handbook*.

ACTIVITY 7 | Describing nouns with adjectives

Combine the related sentences into one sentence. Some words are not used. Use correct capitalization and punctuation.

1. Rob owns a car. The car is red.

Rob owns a red car.

2. I do not like this weather. The weather is cold.

_____

3. Paris is a city in France. This city is beautiful.

_____

4. Ali has a job. The job is new.

_____

5. They like to drink coffee. The coffee is very hot.

_____

6. Nina reads stories. They are funny.

_____

7. My mother grows roses. The roses are big. The roses are beautiful.

_____

8. Juan works for a company. The company is large. The company is international.

_____

9. My grandparents live in a town. It is a farming town. The town is small.

_____

10. Sharon rents a house on Smith Street. The house is white. The house is tiny.

_____

Grammar: Linking Verb + Adjective

A **linking verb** connects the subject to the words after the verb. *Be* is a linking verb. Other linking verbs are related to the five senses: sight, taste, touch, smell, and hearing. If the main verb of a sentence is a linking verb, the adjective comes after the verb.

SUBJECT	LINKING VERB	ADJECTIVE
The boys	are	young.
I	am	sleepy.
That house	is	big.
Justin	looks	ill.
The grapes	taste	delicious.
The hot water	feels	good.
These flowers	smell	sweet.
Sohee's plan	sounds	interesting.
Tony and Ron	seem	nervous.

ACTIVITY 8 | Identifying adjectives

There are ten adjectives in the paragraph. Find and underline them. Circle any linking verbs.

> **WORDS TO KNOW** Paragraph 2.12
>
> **culture:** (n) ideas, activities, and behaviors that are special to a people, country, or region
>
> **dream:** (n) a hope for something

PARAGRAPH 2.12

My Dream Vacation

I have a **dream** to visit Alaska. The weather is beautiful there. I love cold weather. When the temperature is low, I have energy! I also want to visit Alaska because I love nature. Alaska looks so pure[1]. I dream about its amazing snowy mountains. In addition, there are unique[2] animals to see. Finally, I want to learn about the native[3] people of Alaska. Their **culture** sounds very interesting to me. I really want to visit this wonderful state soon.

[1]pure: clean; not dirty or polluted
[2]unique: one of a kind
[3]native: coming from or belonging to a particular place

ACTIVITY 9 | Writing sentences

Look at the photo and read the caption. Write seven to nine sentences about the photo. Use *there is/there are*, prepositional phrases of place, and/or adjectives.

1. The market is in Indonesia.

2. _____

3. _____

4. _____

5. _____

6. _____

7. _____

8. _____

9. _____

Lok Baintan floating market in Indonesia

Sequence Words and Phrases

We use **sequence words and phrases** to show the order of ideas in a paragraph. Notice the sequence words in Paragraph 2.1, "The Best Place to Relax."

> My back porch is my favorite place to relax. **First**, it has a lot of comfortable chairs with soft pillows. . . . My back porch is **also** very quiet. . . . **Finally**, in the evening, I can sit on my porch and watch the sunset.

Some other sequence words and phrases are *next, in addition, then*, and *last*.

ACTIVITY 10 | Ordering sentences

Put the supporting sentences in order from 1 to 8. The topic sentence (TS) is marked for you.

_____ **a.** Doctors say that one hour of exercise each day can keep you in good shape.

_____ **b.** First, you need to eat healthy food.

__TS__ **c.** It is easy to stay healthy if you follow some simple steps.

_____ **d.** This allows your body to rest and become stronger.

_____ **e.** The best types of food to eat are fruits and vegetables.

_____ **f.** Exercise is also good for your mind.

_____ **g.** Finally, you need to find time to relax.

_____ **h.** You should eat a lot of them every day.

_____ **i.** Next, you need to do some exercise.

Grammar: Subject and Object Pronouns

When you write about a topic, using the same noun again and again in your paragraph can make your writing sound repetitive.

> **Alisa** lives in the city. **Alisa** likes the noise and the crowds, but **Alisa** does not like the stress.

> Alisa has **many friends**. She talks to **these friends** every day. She sees **these friends** every weekend.

To make your writing more interesting, replace some nouns with pronouns.

Subject pronouns come before the verb.

SINGULAR SUBJECT PRONOUN		PLURAL SUBJECT PRONOUN	
I	live in Panama.	**We**	live in Panama.
You	work in a bank.	**You**	work in a bank.
He/She/It	is from Turkey.	**They**	are from Turkey.

In the following sentence, the subject pronoun *she* takes the place of *Alisa*.

> **Alisa** lives in the city. **She** likes the noise and crowds, but **she** does not like the stress.

Object pronouns usually come after the verb.

SINGULAR OBJECT PRONOUN		PLURAL OBJECT PRONOUN	
Mona likes	**me.**	Mona likes	**us.**
I know	**you.**	I know	**you.**
Kevin understands	**him/her/it.**	Kevin understands	**them.**

In the following sentence, the object pronoun *them* takes the place of *friends*.

> Alisa has many **friends**. She talks to **them** every day. She sees **them** every weekend.

An object pronoun can also come after a preposition.

	PREPOSITION	OBJECT PRONOUN
Assad walks	with	**me.** **us.**
They give help	to	**you.** **him/her/it.**
Jessica lives	near	**them.**

Only use a pronoun when the noun it is replacing is clear. In the following sentences, it is not clear which noun *they* replaces, *scientists* or *experiments*.

> The scientists do experiments in the lab. **They** are very interesting.

In this case, it is better to use the noun.

> The scientists do experiments in the lab. **These experiments** are interesting.

ACTIVITY 11 | Using subject pronouns

Replace the noun(s) in parentheses with a subject pronoun.

Two Conservationists

Vitor Becker and Clemira Souza are interesting people. Vitor is a scientist.
¹ _____ (Vitor Becker) is married to Clemira. ² _____ (Clemira
Souza) is a professor. ³ _____ (Vitor and Clemira) are also conservationists.
⁴ _____ (Vitor and Clemira) work to protect the rain forest and its animals
in Brazil. ⁵ _____ (Vitor and Clemira) created the Serra Bonita Reserve
on old farmland. ⁶ _____ (The Serra Bonita Reserve) is in the rain forest. ⁷
_____ (The Serra Bonita Reserve) is Vitor and Clemira's home. Scientists and
students visit the Serra Bonita Reserve. ⁸ _____ (The scientists and students)
study the plants and animals of this special part of the rain forest. Tourists also visit Serra
Bonita. ⁹ _____ (The tourists) explore and learn about the reserve. Vitor
and Clemira work hard every day of the week to help these visitors. ¹⁰ _____
(Vitor and Clemira) love their important home in the rain forest.

The Serra Bonita Reserve in Brazil

ACTIVITY 12 | Using object pronouns

Replace the noun(s) in parentheses with an object pronoun.

My Best Friend

My best friend Gretchen is a very interesting woman. I met [1] _____

(Gretchen) ten years ago. She is from Alabama. She comes from a very large family.

She has four brothers and three sisters. She does not live with [2] _____

(her brothers and sisters). They live in Alabama with their parents. Gretchen studies

veterinary medicine[1] in another state. She loves [3] _____ (veterinary medicine)

because she really cares about animals. Gretchen has three pets. She has a cat, a small bird,

and a large horse, Hal. She likes [4] _____ (her pets) all very much. However,

she likes Hal the best. In her free time, Gretchen plays tennis, reads books, and cooks.

I love [5] _____ (Gretchen) like a sister. I hope that our friendship will stay

with [6] _____ (Gretchen and me) for many years.

[1]veterinary medicine: medicine that deals with the care of animals

ACTIVITY 13 | Using pronouns

This paragraph uses the same nouns too many times. Cross out some nouns, and replace them
with subject or object pronouns.

Our Big Move

Andy and I have a busy day today. ~~Andy and I~~ *We* are very excited because we are moving into

a new apartment. Andy and I have many big things to move. I have a large flat screen television.

Andy and I plan to put the television next to the window. Andy's sister and her friends will

help Andy and me move today, too. Andy's sister and her friends will move our large couch

and chairs and put the couch and chairs in front of the television. Finally, Andy's sister and her

friends will move our beds. Our beds may take a long time to move because our beds are so big.

However, Andy and I are not worried because Andy's sister and her friends will help Andy and

me quickly finish everything on our long moving list.

Grammar: Possessive Adjectives

When you want to talk about something that belongs to someone or something, you can use a **possessive adjective**. A possessive adjective answers the question *Whose?* as in *Whose house? Whose books?* and *Whose television?*

A possessive adjective comes before the noun that it describes.

SUBJECT PRONOUN	POSSESSIVE ADJECTIVE	EXAMPLE
I	**my**	**My** <u>house</u> is on Mariposa Avenue.
you	**your**	Do you have **your** <u>ticket</u> for the airplane?
he	**his**	Nick lives with **his** <u>father</u>.
she	**her**	**Her** <u>purse</u> is red and black.
it	**its**	A butterfly moves **its** <u>wings</u> quickly.
we	**our**	We write all **our** <u>papers</u> on a computer.
they	**their**	The students will bring **their** <u>CDs</u>.

For information on possessive pronouns, see the Writer's Handbook.

ACTIVITY 14 | Using possessive adjectives

Fill in each blank with the correct possessive adjective.

> **PARAGRAPH 2.16**
>
> ## Kate and Her Siblings
>
> Kate has a lot of siblings. She has two sisters and one brother.
> ¹ _____ names are Ashley, Julia, and Nick. Ashley and Julia live with
> ² _____ parents. They are high school students. Ashley likes to play
> sports. ³ _____ favorite sport is softball. She is a very good player. Julia
> does not like sports, but she loves music. She plays ⁴ _____ guitar every
> afternoon after school. Ashley and Julia have the same friends. ⁵ _____
> friends go to the same school. ⁶ _____ brother, Nick, is in college.
> ⁷ _____ major is business administration. Kate's brother and sisters are
> all very different, but she loves ⁸ _____ siblings very much.

ACTIVITY 15 | Using subject pronouns and possessive adjectives

Choose the correct subject pronoun or possessive adjective.

PARAGRAPH 2.17

My Grandmother

A very important person in ¹ (I / my) life is ² (I / my) grandmother. ³ (She / Her) name is Evelyn Anna Kratz. ⁴ (She / Her) life is very interesting. ⁵ (She / Her) is 89 years old. ⁶ (She / Her) comes from Poland. ⁷ (She / Her) speaks English well, but ⁸ (she / her) first language is Polish. My grandmother comes from a large family. ⁹ (She / Her) has three sisters. ¹⁰ (They / Their) names are Karina, Dorota, and Maria. ¹¹ (I / My) grandmother has one brother, too. ¹² (He / His) name is Peter. When ¹³ (they / them) talk about ¹⁴ (they / their) lives, ¹⁵ (I / My) love to listen. In ¹⁶ (I / my) opinion, they are the most interesting stories in the world.

Parts of a Paragraph: The Concluding Sentence

In addition to a topic sentence and body, a good paragraph has a **concluding sentence**. The concluding sentence:

- ends the paragraph with a final thought
- often expresses the same idea as the topic sentence using different words
- does not give any new information about the topic

Look at the topic sentences and concluding sentences from a few paragraphs in this unit. Notice how they express the same ideas in different ways. Words that are important to the topic may be repeated.

TOPIC SENTENCE	CONCLUDING SENTENCE
My back porch is my favorite place to relax.	I can relax in many places, but my back porch is the best.
The Shanghai Tower is an amazing building.	The Shanghai Tower is amazing inside and out.
I have a dream to visit Alaska.	I really want to visit this wonderful state soon.

ACTIVITY 16 | Analyzing concluding sentences

Write the topic sentence and concluding sentence from each paragraph indicated. Then underline the similar information. Discuss your answers with a partner.

1. Paragraph 2.3

Topic sentence: _____

Concluding sentence: _____

2. Paragraph 2.4

Topic sentence: _____

Concluding sentence: _____

3. Paragraph 2.5

Topic sentence: _____

Concluding sentence: _____

ACTIVITY 17 | Identifying concluding sentences

Read each paragraph and choose the best concluding sentence.

> **WORDS TO KNOW** Paragraphs 2.18 to 2.19
>
> **careful:** (adj) aware of danger; cautious   **celebrate:** (v) to do something to mark a special event

PARAGRAPH 2.18

Buying a Car

Buying a car requires **careful** planning. First, you must decide to buy a new or a used car. New cars can be expensive, but they are reliable. Used cars are cheaper, but they often need repairs. You must also decide on what type of car to buy. You can research different types of cars on the Internet to help you choose. The final decision is where to buy your car. Some places charge you more money than others.

a. It is important to think about all of these things when you are buying a car.

b. The most important thing is the kind of car that you want to buy.

c. You can buy your new car from a friend or a car dealer.

People enjoy Hanami in Kyoto, Japan.

PARAGRAPH 2.19

Hanami

Hanami, or flower viewing, is a popular Japanese tradition. Every spring, thousands of cherry trees bloom all over Japan. For two weeks during Hanami, friends and families gather in parks and the countryside to see the beautiful flowers and **celebrate** the beginning of spring. People make a lot of food and have picnics under the trees. There is a lot of music and dancing, and large groups of people walk through the parks together. The celebrations often go into the night.

a. People like to be with their family and friends during Hanami.
b. Looking at flowers during Hanami is interesting.
c. Hanami is a Japanese custom many people love.

PARAGRAPH 2.20

Mondays

I hate Mondays for many reasons. One reason is work. I get up early to go to work on Mondays. After a weekend of fun and relaxation, I do not like to do this. Another reason that I do not like Mondays is that I have three meetings every Monday. These meetings last a long time, and they are extremely boring. Traffic is also a big problem on Mondays. There are more cars on the road on Mondays. Drivers are in a hurry, and I must be more careful than usual when I drive.

a. Mondays are worse than Tuesdays, but they are better than Sundays.
b. I do not like meetings on Mondays.
c. These are just a few reasons why I do not like Mondays.

ACTIVITY 18 | Writing a paragraph

Look back at Activity 10. Write the sentences in paragraph order. Remember to indent the topic sentence. Then write a concluding sentence for the paragraph.

Staying Healthy

An AntiGravity yoga class in Boston, USA

BUILDING BETTER VOCABULARY

ACTIVITY 19 | Word associations

Circle the word or phrase that is more closely related to the bold word on the left.

1.	amazing	very boring	very interesting
2.	bother	help	annoy
3.	careful	cautious	worried
4.	celebrate	do an everyday activity	do something special
5.	compete	try to finish	try to win
6.	danger	something difficult	something unsafe
7.	during	at the time	after the time
8.	extremely	rarely	really
9.	fan	love	hate
10.	plan	finish	prepare

ACTIVITY 20 | Collocations

Fill in the blank with the word that most naturally completes the phrase.

culture	dream	explain	patient	relax

1. be _____ while waiting

2. clearly _____ the directions

3. _____ after a long day

4. my biggest _____

5. ancient Chinese _____

| accident | check | explore | taste | traffic |

6. _____ delicious

7. _____ the dictionary

8. _____ new places

9. a serious car _____

10. heavy _____

ACTIVITY 21 | Word forms

Complete each sentence with the correct word form. Use the correct form of the nouns and verbs.

NOUN	VERB	ADJECTIVE	SENTENCE PRACTICE
comfort	comfort	comfortable	1. My new dress is extremely _____. 2. Parents often _____ crying children.
connection	connect	connected	3. People can _____ with each other easily through the Internet. 4. I study at this library all the time because the WiFi _____ here is very good.
damage	damage	damaged	5. High-heeled shoes _____ wooden floors. 6. The _____ car does not work.
energy	energize	energetic	7. Young children can be very _____. 8. Riders need a lot of _____ to complete a race.
organization	organize	organized	9. There are many ways to _____ a closet. 10. My boss is a very _____ woman.

ACTIVITY 22 | Vocabulary in writing

Choose five words from Words to Know. Write a complete sentence with each word.

1. _____

2. _____

3. _____

4. _____

5. _____

BUILDING BETTER SENTENCES

ACTIVITY 23 | Editing from teacher comments

Read the teacher's comments. Then rewrite the paragraph correctly on a separate piece of paper.

PARAGRAPH 2.21

Aspirin

Aspirin is an incredible type of medicine. This small white pill is not a <u>drug new</u>. We do *word order* not know exactly why or how it works. <u>however</u>, millions of people use aspirin every day. *capitalization* They take <u>them</u> for many reasons. Aspirin<u>_</u>good for headaches, colds, and pain. <u>They</u> can help *incorrect pronoun* *missing linking verb* *incorrect pronoun* with so many different health problems. <u>a</u>spirin is a simple medicine, but it <u>so important is</u>. *capitalization* *word order*

A climber with a headache from altitude sickness

ACTIVITY 24 | Editing sentences

Find and correct the errors. The number in parentheses tells how many errors each sentence has.

1. Amal a student at Seattle Community College. (1)

2. There is 15 floors in this building. (1)

3. Jim's backpack difficult to carry. (1)

4. Me shirt favorite is not clean. (2)

5. Mysteries are a popular type of book (1)

6. The sun damages skin unprotected. (1)

7. The Shanghai Tower a building tall. (2)

8. Is not raining today. (1)

9. There are a lot of information about the project (2)

10. Everyone loves him beautiful smile. (1)

ACTIVITY 25 | Combining sentences

Combine the ideas into one sentence. You may change the word forms, but do not change or omit any ideas. There may be more than one answer. See Unit 1 for more information.

1. There is a meeting.
   The meeting is important.
   The meeting in on a calendar.
   The calendar is Linh's.

   _____

2. Carlos rides a bike to work.
   The bike belongs to Carlos.
   Carlos rides the bike every day.

   _____

3. I have friends.
   These friends are new.
   These friends are in my English class.

   _____

WRITING

ACTIVITY 26 | Writing a paragraph

Write an original paragraph. Follow the instructions.

- Answer the questions in the chart below. Use complete sentences or notes.
- Use at least two vocabulary words or phrases from the unit.
- Copy your sentences into paragraph form on a separate piece of paper. Underline vocabulary from the unit.
- Give your paragraph a title.

Topic Sentence	**1.** Who is the most interesting person you know? (This is your topic sentence.) *The most interesting person I know is* _____
Body	**2.** Why is this person interesting? List three reasons. Give an example to support each reason. Use adjectives in your descriptions. (These are your supporting sentences.) Reason 1: _____ Example 1: _____ Reason 2: _____ Example 2: _____ Reason 3: _____ Example 3: _____
Concluding Sentence	**3.** Write a concluding sentence that gives information similar to the information in your topic sentence. Use an adjective other than *interesting*. _____

Editing

After you finish writing, check your work for errors. Use the checklist below to help you.

- ☐ The paragraph has a title.
- ☐ I wrote a topic sentence and a concluding sentence. They are connected in meaning.
- ☐ I indented the first line of the paragraph.
- ☐ My supporting sentences are related to the topic.
- ☐ I used adjectives in my descriptions.
- ☐ I used subject and object pronouns to add variety.
- ☐ I used possessive adjectives to show ownership.

ACTIVITY 27 | Peer Editing

Exchange books with a partner and look at Activity 26. Read your partner's paragraph. Then use Peer Editing Form 2 in the *Writer's Handbook* to help you comment on your partner's paragraph.

Additional Topics for Writing

Choose one or more of the topics to write about. Follow your teacher's directions.

TOPIC 1: Review your Freewrite response for this unit. Who are you a fan of? Why do you like this person?

TOPIC 2: What are the qualities of a good friend? Why are these qualities important for a good friend to have?

TOPIC 3: Write about your phone, computer, or other electronic device. How often do you use it? What do you use it for? Do you like it? Why or why not?

TOPIC 4: Write about your favorite kind of entertainment. Why do you like this entertainment? How do you feel when you experience it?

TOPIC 5: Write about something you do not like. What is it? Give three reasons why you do not like it. Provide examples to support your reasons.

TEST PREP

You should spend about 25 minutes on this task. Write a paragraph with six to ten sentences.

> **TIP**
>
> Before you start to write, read the question carefully. Then write a strong topic sentence that answers the question. Use words from the question in your topic sentence. The rest of the paragraph should explain or give reasons to support your topic sentence.

Some people believe that success in life comes from taking risks or chances. Others believe that success results from careful planning. In your opinion, what does success come from? Use specific reasons and examples to support your answer.

Remember to indent the first line of your paragraph. Include a topic sentence, supporting sentences, and a concluding sentence. Check your work for correct use of pronouns and adjectives.

Aisholpan Nurgaiv is the first female eagle hunter in her family, and the first female to compete in and win the Golden Eagle Festival in Mongolia.

OBJECTIVES

- Write sentences in the simple present
- Write simple and compound sentences
- Use *and*, *but*, and *so* in compound sentences
- Use *a*, *an*, *the*, and Ø article
- Write an original paragraph

3 | Writing about the Present

FREEWRITE | Look at the photo and read the caption. What is a sport or hobby that you like to do? Describe it.

ELEMENTS OF GREAT WRITING

Using the Simple Present

The **simple present** is one way to discuss the present. It is very common in academic writing. We use the simple present to describe:

- regular activities or habits

  Dr. Jones begins his days by visiting patients.
  Carla drinks two cups of coffee every day.

- facts or things that are generally true

  Earth revolves around the Sun.
  The people of Iceland are friendly and helpful.

- a process (how to make or do something)

  Next, the artist prepares his materials.
  Finally, the delicious meal is ready to serve.

ACTIVITY 1 | Analyzing sentences

Identify whether each sentence is describing a *habit* (H), *fact* (F), or *process* (P).

1. _____ Boston, USA, has many colleges and universities.

2. _____ After you finish your paragraph, you should edit it.

3. _____ Water freezes at 0°C.

4. _____ It is possible to build a camera with materials from your home in a few steps.

5. _____ My mother often wears a beautiful pair of gold earrings.

6. _____ One year on Neptune lasts about 165 Earth years.

7. _____ Every weekday, Samantha drives to her English class.

8. _____ Next, add milk and sugar to the coffee.

9. _____ Arthur always eats popcorn when he watches a movie.

10. _____ My laptop computer has a beautiful blue cover.

Grammar: The Simple Present Affirmative

The simple present affirmative has two forms: the base form and the -s form.

SUBJECT	VERB	OTHER INFORMATION
I/You/We/They	**like** **wash** **carry**	to go to the beach. the dishes in the sink. suitcases to the airport.
He/She/It	**likes** **washes** **carries**	

For most verbs, add *s* to make the -*s* form. However, when the verb ends
- in *ss*, *sh*, *ch*, *z*, or *x*, add *es* (teach → teaches)
- in a consonant + *y*, change the *y* to *i* and add *es* (cry → cries)
- in a vowel + *y*, add *s* (play → plays)

The verbs *have*, *do*, and *go* have irregular -*s* forms.

SUBJECT	VERB + OTHER INFORMATION
He/She/It	**has** a new friend. **does** exercise. **goes** to school.

Remember that the verb *be* has three forms in the simple present.

SUBJECT	VERB + OTHER INFORMATION
I	**am** a student.
You/We/They	**are** on vacation.
He/She/It	**is** smart.

In informal writing, you can use contractions. A contraction is a shortened form of two words combined with an apostrophe ('). Do not use contractions in academic writing.

I am = I'm   he is = he's
you are = you're   she is = she's
we are = we're   it is = it's
they are = they're

Remember to use the -*s* form with a third-person singular subject.
- ✓ He **calls** his parents every day.
- ✗ He call his parents every day.

ACTIVITY 2 | Using the simple present affirmative

Fill in each blank with the simple present form of the verb in parentheses.

WORDS TO KNOW Paragraph 3.1

immediately: (adv) right now

patient: (n) a person cared for by a doctor or nurse

PARAGRAPH 3.1

Dr. Sindi's Test

Dr. Hayat Sindi [1]_____ (have) a portable[1] test for liver[2] problems.
The test is made of paper and [2]_____ (be) very small—the size of a
stamp you use to mail a letter. This [3]_____ (make) it cheap and easy
to bring to people in remote[3] areas of the world. When doctors [4]_____
(travel) to these places, they can take hundreds of the tests with them. They [5]
_____ (give) the tests to people and [6]_____ (see)
the results **immediately**. So they [7]_____ (be) able to help sick people in
their own villages. Dr. Sindi's amazing test [8]_____ (make) life easier for
doctors and their **patients** around the world.

[1]portable: capable of being carried or moved around
[2]liver: the part of your body that helps to clean your blood
[3]remote: far away; difficult to reach

Dr. Hayat Sindi,
a biotechnologist and
entrepreneur from
Saudi Arabia

ACTIVITY 3 | Using the simple present affirmative

Fill in each blank with the simple present form of a verb in the word bank. Some verbs are used more than once.

be	come	have	love	play	practice	speak

PARAGRAPH 3.2

My Classmates

My classmates come from all over the world. José ¹_____ from

Spain, so he ²_____ Spanish. Wonbin, Hyun-Ju, and Hee-Young

³_____ Korean, but they ⁴_____ from different cities.

Yuri ⁵_____ from Ukraine. He ⁶_____ English all the

time and ⁷_____ a great accent. The Al-Ahmad brothers

⁸_____ from Oman, and they ⁹_____ soccer very well.

I ¹⁰_____ from Italy, and I ¹¹_____ to sing in class. We

¹²_____ all very different, and that makes our class interesting.

ACTIVITY 4 | Changing from singular to plural

Read the paragraph. Then follow the steps to rewrite it on a separate piece of paper.

1. Change the subject of the sentences from *Jim* to *Jim and Matt.*
2. Make any necessary changes to subjects, nouns, pronouns, and verb forms.

> **WORDS TO KNOW** Paragraph 3.3
>
> **hurry:** (v) to be quick
> **routine:** (n) things that someone does regularly
> **stressful:** (adj) causing worry and tension
> **temporary:** (adj) for a short time

PARAGRAPH 3.3

Jim's Daily Routine

Jim is a very busy student. Every morning, he wakes up at 7:00 a.m., gets ready, and then **hurries** off to school. He studies engineering at City College. He attends school for six hours every day. After school, he goes to his job at a clothes store. After his job, he goes home, eats a quick dinner, studies, and does his homework. Jim knows that his **routine** is **stressful**. He also knows that the routine is **temporary** because he will graduate soon.

ACTIVITY 5 | Editing a paragraph

The paragraph has six missing *be* verbs and three missing *have* verbs. Find and correct them.

> **WORDS TO KNOW** Paragraph 3.4
>
> **destination:** (n) where someone is going
> **flow:** (v) to move smoothly
>
> **miss:** (v) to not participate in something
> **national:** (adj) related to a country

PARAGRAPH 3.4

The City of Budapest

Budapest, Hungary, ~~is~~ one of the most interesting cities in Europe. First, it many interesting tourist **destinations**. One example the Danube River. It **flows** through the middle of the city, and it a long connection with human history. Budapest also beautiful architecture[1]. Buda Castle a World Heritage Site[2]. In addition, there a long history of traditional food in Hungary. There many **national** dishes. One of the most popular goulash soup. When you travel to Europe, do not **miss** a visit to Budapest.

[1]architecture: the style or design of buildings
[2]World Heritage Site: a place that is important to culture, history, or science

A view of Buda Castle across the Danube River

ACTIVITY 6 | Writing about pictures

Look at the pictures. Then complete Paragraph 3.5 with the correct word, phrase, or sentence.

WORDS TO KNOW Paragraph 3.5

certainly: (adv) for sure

whole: (adj) all of something

PARAGRAPH 3.5

One Family's Morning Routine

The Lee family is very busy on weekday mornings. Every morning, Susan Lee, the oldest child, wakes up and ¹_____ for the **whole** family. She loves to do that. When the food is ready, everyone ²_____. The kids eat their breakfast quickly. After they eat, Susan's father and mother ³_____ _____. At 8:30 a.m., ⁴_____ _____. Mr. Lee drives the kids to school before he goes to work. ⁵_____. A few minutes later, ⁶_____. The Lees **certainly** do a lot before their day at work and school begins.

WRITER'S NOTE *There are* vs. *They are*

Be careful not to confuse *There are* and *They are*.

There are shows that something exists. A plural subject comes after *are*.
They are is the beginning of a sentence with the subject *They*.

✓ **There are** five people in my family.
✗ They are five people in my family.
✓ I speak two languages. **They are** English and Arabic.
✗ I speak two languages. There are English and Arabic.

ACTIVITY 7 | Choosing *they are* or *there are*

Choose *they are* or *there are* to complete the paragraph.

WORDS TO KNOW Paragraph 3.6

admire: (v) to like
well-known: (adj) famous

space: (n) where the moon, stars, and other planets are

The Space Needle in Seattle, Washington, USA

PARAGRAPH 3.6

Amazing Tourist Towers

[1](They are / There are) many famous World's Fair[1] towers all over the world. [2](They are / There are) popular tourist destinations. The most **well-known** is the Eiffel Tower from the 1889 fair in Paris, France. [3](They are / There are) beautiful lights on the tower at night, and tourists often ride boats on the Seine River to **admire** them. Another famous tower is the Space Needle in Seattle, USA, from the 1962 World's Fair. [4](They are / There are) many people who think the top of the Space Needle looks like something from **space**. In Daejeon, South Korea, tourists love to visit the Tower of Grand Light from the 1993 World's Fair. The tower is now part of a giant amusement park[2], and [5](they are / there are) pools, movie theaters, and exciting rides. [6](They are / There are) always crowded with people enjoying themselves. These are only a few of the amazing World's Fair towers.

[1]World's Fair: an international exhibition of the achievements of different nations
[2]amusement park: a large outdoor area with rides, games, shows, and food and drink

ACTIVITY 8 | Using *they are* or *there are*

Complete each sentence with *They are* or *There are*.

1. _____ too many questions on this test.

2. _____ happy to see us today.

3. _____ at the doctor.

4. _____ many different ways to study English.

5. _____ some apples in the kitchen.

6. _____ at the store right now.

7. _____ my favorite subjects.

8. _____ errors in your paragraph.

9. _____ many great teachers at our school.

10. _____ excited about Mark's party.

Grammar: The Simple Present Negative

To make negative statements in the simple present, use *do not* and *does not* before the base form of the verb.

SUBJECT	DO NOT/DOES NOT	BASE FORM OF VERB
I/You/We/They	**do not**	work.
He/She/It	**does not**	understand. listen.

To make negative statements with *be*, use *not* after *am/is/are*.

SUBJECT	FORM OF BE + NOT	
I	**am not**	
You/We/They	**are not**	at home.
He/She/It	**is not**	

In informal writing, you can use these contractions:

do not = don't   is not = isn't
does not = doesn't   are not = aren't

ACTIVITY 9 | Using the simple present negative and affirmative

The sentences below are false. With a partner, rewrite each sentence using the negative form for the verb to make it true. Then write a correct affirmative sentence about the topic. The first one has been done for you.

1. Borscht is a food from England. *Borscht is not a food from England. It is the national dish of Ukraine.*

2. The capital of Japan is Osaka. _____

3. Soccer is the most popular sport in the United States. _____

4. Water freezes at 50 degrees Fahrenheit. _____

5. Angel Falls is in Brazil. _____

6. Seattle and Dallas are cities in France. _____

7. Thailand is a European country. _____

8. Coffee plants grow naturally in Norway. _____

9. The Great Pyramids are in Spain. _____

10. Global warming means the Earth's temperature is going down. _____

11. Canada is near the equator. _____

12. There are four Latin languages. _____

Grammar: Simple and Compound Sentences

Simple Sentences

A **simple sentence** has at least one subject and one verb. It can have a subject-verb combination that has more than one subject and/or more than one verb.

Notice the different subject-verb combinations possible in simple sentences.

SUBJECT	VERB
Japan	**imports** oil from Saudi Arabia.
Japan and Germany	**import** oil from Saudi Arabia.
Japan	**imports** oil and **exports** cars.
Japan and Germany	**import** oil and **export** cars.

Compound Sentences

A **compound sentence** is two simple sentences that are joined by a comma and a connector (such as *and*). If both sentences have the same subject, replace the second with a pronoun.

SIMPLE SENTENCE 1	CONNECTOR	SIMPLE SENTENCE 2
Japan and Germany import oil	**, and**	Saudi Arabia imports vegetables.
Jack likes Italian food	**, but**	Fatima and Juliana prefer Thai food.
Abbie watches TV at night	**, so**	**she** does not finish her homework on time.
For vacation, we camp in the mountains	**, or**	**we** relax on the beach.

The **connector** in a compound sentence is called a coordinating conjunction. It shows the relationship between the two simple sentences.

CONNECTOR	MEANING
and	adds information
but	adds contrasting (different) information
so	gives the result of the event or information in the first sentence

ACTIVITY 10 | Identifying sentence types

Circle the subject(s) and underline the verb(s) in each sentence. Then write S for *simple sentence* or CD for *compound sentence*.

1. _____CD_____ (Japan's flag) <u>is</u> red and white, and (Canada's flag) <u>is</u> also red and white.

2. _____S_____ (Japan and Canada) <u>have</u> the same two colors in their flags.

3. _____ The weather is bad, but the pilot plans to leave on time.

4. _____ It is extremely hot in Abu Dhabi during the summer.

5. _____ The Martellus Map of Europe, Africa, and Asia is over five hundred years old.

6. _____ The Atacama Desert receives almost no rain, so it is the driest desert in the world.

7. _____ Students in many countries take college entrance exams, but they do not like it.

8. _____ January, March, May, July, August, October, and December have 31 days.

9. _____ The Olympic rings represent the flags of every country, so they are blue, yellow, red, black, and green.

10. _____ Baseball and golf are popular sports to watch and play.

11. _____ Some people prefer gold jewelry, but others prefer silver jewelry.

12. _____ Research requires time, patience, and determination.

WRITER'S NOTE Writing Lists of Words

When you write a sentence that contains a list of three or more items:

- put a comma after each item except the last one
- make sure all the words in the list are the same part of speech, such as all verbs or all nouns
- try not to make the list longer than three or four items

Lucas will visit <u>London</u>, <u>Paris</u>, <u>Rome</u>, and <u>Prague</u> next year.
(n   n   n   n)

Andrea has <u>pink</u>, <u>yellow</u>, and <u>white</u> roses in her garden.
(adj   adj   adj)

ACTIVITY 11 | Identifying commas in a list

Look back at Activity 10. Underline the four sentences that contain a list of three or more items.

ACTIVITY 12 | Writing compound sentences

Combine each pair of simple sentences into one compound sentence. Use *and*, *but* or *so*. There may be more than one answer.

1. Seher lives in Turkey. Her sister lives in Canada.

   _____

2. Carlos works on Saturday. He cannot come to the movies with us.

   _____

3. We go to school every day. We play tennis on weekends.

   _____

4. Luis and Kathy are related. They are not brother and sister.

   _____

5. Hurricanes begin in the Atlantic Ocean. Typhoons begin in the Pacific.

   _____

6. Some people think tomatoes are fruit. Other people think they are vegetables.

   _____

7. Ali is a medical student. He takes a lot of science classes.

   _____

8. Maja usually goes to bed early. She is up late tonight.

   _____

9. Jiang does not like coffee. He drinks tea.

   _____

10. It is quiet at the library. Students like to study there.

    _____

11. My parents have a telephone in their home. I only have a cell phone.

    _____

12. Some fish live in fresh water. Some fish live in salt water.

    _____

ACTIVITY 13 | Editing a paragraph

The paragraph has ten errors. Find and correct them.

six simple present errors   two connecting word errors   two comma errors

> **WORDS TO KNOW** Paragraph 3.7
>
> **gym:** (n) a place for physical exercise or sports practice   **typical:** (adj) average; normal
> **individual:** (adj) different from others; separate

A gymnast competes on the parallel bars.

PARAGRAPH 3.7

Not an Average Teenager

Steven Mills not is your **typical** teenager. Steven is a competitive gymnast, or he want to compete in the Olympics. He wake up at 5:00 in the morning every day and he practices before school. He jogs to the **gym,** but he practices gymnastics for two hours. Then he eats a healthy breakfast, and he gets ready for school. Steven go to school from 8:30 in the morning until 2:00 in the afternoon. After school, he returns to the gym for **individual** practice with his coach. When practice finish at 6:00 in the evening, Steven returns home. He eats dinner, do his homework and talks with his family. Steven is in bed early to be ready to work hard again the next day.

Grammar: Using *A* and *An* or Ø

A and *an* are called **indefinite articles.** We use articles with nouns.

There are two types of nouns in English: count and non-count. Count nouns can be counted. They have a singular form (*phone, person*) and a plural form (*phones, people*). Non-count nouns are not countable. They have only one form (*money, information*).

A singular count noun cannot stand alone. We use an article or another word before it, such as *this, that,* or a possessive adjective (*my, your, his,* etc.). Use:

- *a* or *an* before a singular count noun when its meaning is general (not specific)

  We want to buy **a** <u>house</u> in the future.

- *a* before a singular count noun that begins with a consonant sound

  a break / **a** dream / **a** horse / **a** uniform

- *an* before a singular count noun that begins with a vowel sound

  an animal / **an** engineer / **an** honor / **an** uncle

When there is an adjective before a singular count noun, use the beginning sound of the adjective, not the noun, to choose *a* or *an*.

- ✓ Our friends attend **an** <u>excellent</u> school.
- ✗ Our friends attend a excellent school.

We do not use *a* or *an* before plural count nouns or non-count nouns.

- ✓ <u>Computers</u> are part of everyone's life. (Ø article)
- ✗ A computers are part of everyone's life.

For more information on using *a* or *an* and a list of common non-count nouns, see the *Writer's Handbook*.

ACTIVITY 14 | Choosing *a*, *an*, or Ø

Write each noun or noun phrase in the correct column.

accidents	extra pencil	information	solution
computers	happy memory	money	umbrella
daily activity	hour	object	university

A	An	Ø

ACTIVITY 15 | Editing sentences

Each sentence is missing *a* or *an*. Add the correct indefinite article to each one.

1. My father has stressful job

2. You have exam today.

3. Our teacher gives us project every week.

4. There is large cake for my son's birthday.

5. His mother is amazing woman.

6. We have test in this class every week.

7. Their sister is excellent cook.

8. You can buy e-book on that website.

Grammar: Using *The*

The is called the **definite article**. Use *the*:

- before a singular count noun, plural count noun, or non-count noun when its meaning is specific (not general)

  I do not have my keys, so I am locked out of **the** house.

- for the second (and third, fourth, etc.) time you talk about something

  I have a sweater and a coat. **The** sweater is made of wool, but **the** coat is made of leather.

- when the noun you are referring to is unique—there is only one

  The Hubble Space Telescope takes incredible pictures of outer space.
  The Taj Mahal is a beautiful monument.

For more information on using *the*, see the *Writer's Handbook*.

ACTIVITY 16 | Using *a, an, the,* and Ø

Choose the correct article to complete the paragraph.

> **WORDS TO KNOW** Paragraph 3.8
>
> **can afford:** (phr) to have enough money   **create:** (v) to make something

Shipping containers used as student dormitories in Amsterdam, the Netherlands

PARAGRAPH 3.8

An Exciting Way to Recycle

[1](A / The) company in the Netherlands is recycling in [2](a / an) new and exciting way. [3](A / The) company is changing old shipping containers into new buildings. First, it cleans [4](Ø / the) containers. Then it adds [5](Ø / a) new floors, [6](Ø / the) windows, and electricity to each one. After that, the outside of [7](Ø / the) new building is painted [8](a / the) bright color. Often, [9](a / the) company connects containers to **create** [10](a / an) apartment building or student dormitory. Some containers even become stores. In the end, it costs much less money to make [11](Ø / a) new building from [12](an / Ø) old container, so more people **can afford** to buy or rent one. Making shipping containers into new buildings adds about one hundred years of life to shipping containers, and is [13](an / the) amazing way to recycle.

ACTIVITY 17 | Using the simple present and articles

Choose the correct form of the verb. Then add an article (*a*, *an*, *the*) where necessary.

1. Robert always (go / goes) to beach near his house.

2. Laura's parents (visit / visits) their friends in India once a year.

3. We (have / has) grammar test now.

4. The weather (is / are) very nice for picnic today.

5. Brad often (eat / eats) apples for snack.

6. I (lend / lends) you pencil all the time.

7. This computer (do not work / does not work) anymore.

8. Ian (buy / buys) cup of coffee during his afternoon break.

9. Nicholas and Karla (take / takes) classes at Seattle Community College.

10. My dad (drive / drives) me to airport when I travel.

BUILDING BETTER VOCABULARY

WORDS TO KNOW

admire (v)	flow (v)	miss (v)	stressful (adj) AW
can afford (phr)	gym (n)	national (adj)	temporary (adj) AW
certainly (adv)	hurry (v)	patient (n)	typical (adj)
create (v) AW	immediately (adv)	routine (n)	well-known (adj)
destination (n) AW	individual (adj) AW	space (n)	whole (adj)

ACTIVITY 18 | Word associations

Circle the word or phrase that is more closely related to the bold word on the left.

1. admire	dislike	like
2. certainly	surely	usually
3. gym	exercise	rest
4. immediately	later	now
5. individual	together	separate
6. national	country	world
7. patient	hospital	supermarket
8. typical	normal	rare
9. well-known	famous	healthy
10. whole	all of	none of

ACTIVITY 19 | Collocations

Fill in the blank with the word that most naturally completes the phrase.

flow	routine	space	temporary	well-known

1. be in outer _____

2. a _____ author

3. a boring _____

4. rivers _____

5. a _____ solution

| admire | can afford | miss | popular | stressful |

6. a _____ job

7. _____ a meeting

8. a _____ destination

9. _____ someone

10. _____ to buy something

ACTIVITY 20 | Word forms

Complete each sentence with the correct word form. Use the correct form of the nouns and verbs.

NOUN	VERB	ADJECTIVE	SENTENCES
admiration	admire	admiring	**1.** Many people _____ the view from the top of Jebel Hafeet in the United Arab Emirates. **2.** I have a lot of _____ for Olympic athletes.
creation	create	creative	**3.** Artists are _____ people. **4.** The _____ of a new app requires a lot of work.
flow	flow	flowing	**5.** Water _____ down my street after it rains heavily. **6.** It is relaxing to listen to the gentle _____ of the river.
hurry	hurry	hurried	**7.** After work, people are always in a big _____ to get home. **8.** I need to _____ to catch the bus.
stress	stress	stressful	**9.** Don't _____ about the homework assignment. It's easy. **10.** Yuka has a lot of _____ at her job.

ACTIVITY 21 | Vocabulary in writing

Choose five words from Words to Know. Write a complete sentence with each word.

1. _____

2. _____

3. _____

4. _____

5. _____

BUILDING BETTER SENTENCES

ACTIVITY 22 | Editing sentences

Find and correct the errors. The number in parentheses tells how many errors each sentence has.

1. Elephant are native to africa and Asia. (2)

2. The coffee is hot, but you must be careful. (1)

3. The scientists does not have an assistant. (1)

4. Tourists must take boat to visit Statue of Liberty. (2)

5. Me aunt drinks cup of coffee every morning. (2)

6. Many bird fly thousands of miles in the spring. (1)

7. You do not want to be late for test so you must hurry to class. (2)

8. Patient needs to exercise and eat well every day. (1)

9. There are a lot of people leaving the stadium, or they are happy about the final score. (1)

10. Please give you test to teacher. (2)

ACTIVITY 23 | Writing sentences

Write an original sentence using the words listed.

1. (miss/important)

_____

2. (typical/tradition)

_____

3. (always/practice)

_____

4. (extremely/stressful)

_____

5. (attend/well-known)

_____

ACTIVITY 24 | Combining sentences

Combine the ideas into one sentence. You may change the word forms, but do not change or omit any ideas. There may be more than one answer.

1. (HINT: Use a connector.)
Cheetahs have spots.
Leopards have spots.
The spots create patterns.
The patterns are different.

_____

_____

2. (HINT: Use a connector.)
You can see polar bears in Alaska, USA.
You can see grizzly bears in Alaska, USA.
You can see panda bears in south central China.

_____

_____

3. (HINT: Use a connector.)
Miguel wants to be a professional soccer player.
Miguel practices soccer.
Miguel does this every day.

_____

_____

WRITING

ACTIVITY 25 | Writing a paragraph

Think about your favorite activity. Then follow these steps to write a paragraph about it on a separate piece of paper. Put a check (✓) next to each step as you complete it. Use at least one compound sentence and two of the vocabulary words and phrases presented in the unit. Underline the unit vocabulary you use.

1. _____ In your first sentence, write: _____ *is my favorite activity*. Fill in the blank with the name of the activity you like.

2. _____ In your next sentence, write the first reason you like the activity. Next, write a sentence with an explanation about why you like it.

3. _____ In the next sentence, write the second reason that you like the activity. Next, write a sentence with an explanation for this reason.

4. _____ In the next sentence, write the final reason that you like the activity. Next, write a sentence with an explanation for this reason.

5. _____ In the last sentence, write: *These are some of the reasons why I like* _____.

Editing

After you finish your writing, check your work for errors. Use the checklist below to help you.

- ☐ Each sentence has a subject and a verb.
- ☐ I used the base form and *-s* form of verbs correctly.
- ☐ I used at least one compound sentence.
- ☐ I used commas in compound sentences and lists.
- ☐ I included the four main parts of a paragraph and a title.

ACTIVITY 26 | Peer editing

Exchange papers from Activity 25 with a partner. Read your partner's paragraph. Then use Peer Editing Form 2 in the *Writer's Handbook* to help you comment on your partner's paragraph.

Additional Topics for Writing

Choose one or more of the topics to write about. Follow your teacher's directions.

TOPIC 1: Look at the photo on pages 58–59. Hunting with eagles is a national tradition in Mongolia. What sport or hobby is a national tradition in your country? Describe it.

TOPIC 2: Write about something you want to learn, such as planting a garden. Why do you want to learn it? What are the steps for learning it? Do you think it is a hard thing to learn? Why or why not?

TOPIC 3: Write about an interesting career. Include one specific type of job in this career. Write about the duties of the job and why it is interesting.

TOPIC 4: Write about your favorite app. What is it called? What does it do? How does it work? How is your life different with this app?

TOPIC 5: Write about something that you do *not* enjoy doing but have to do. Why don't you like doing it? Why do you have to do it? What happens if you don't do this activity?

TEST PREP

You should spend about 25 minutes on this task. Write a paragraph with six to ten sentences.

Some people prefer to travel with a companion. Others prefer to travel alone. Which do you prefer? Use two or three specific reasons and examples to support your answer.

Use the simple present in your paragraph. Include one or two compound sentences by combining two simple sentences with a comma and the connectors and, but, or so. Use articles as necessary.

> **TIP**
>
> It is important for your writing to look like a paragraph. Be sure to indent the first sentence. Write the rest of the sentences from margin to margin. Leave an appropriate amount of space after your periods. These small details make your paragraph easier to read and understand.

4 | Writing about the Past

OBJECTIVES
- Write sentences in the simple past
- Use past time words and phrases
- Use adverbs of manner

National Geographic
Explorer Aalaa Al Shamahi,
a paleoanthropologist and
comedian, holds a copy of
a Neanderthal skull at
University College London.

FREEWRITE | Look at the photo and read the caption. What do you think of this photo?
What are some funny things you did in the past?

ELEMENTS OF GREAT WRITING

Using the Simple Past

The **simple past** is one way to write about the past. It is common in academic writing. We use the simple past to:

- write about recent or historical events

    The L Tower in Toronto, Canada, opened in 2015.

- tell a narrative, or story, that is real or imagined

    The team's journey to the championship was a difficult one.

- describe the events in a person's life

    As a young man, Mahatma Gandhi worked as a lawyer.

- report on the result of an experiment

    The cell divided several times.

ACTIVITY 1 | Analyzing a paragraph

Read the paragraph. Then answer the questions that follow.

WORDS TO KNOW Paragraph 4.1

invention: (n) something created for the first time
organization: (n) a group that works for a specific goal

prize: (n) a reward for winning something
suffering: (n) mental or physical pain

PARAGRAPH 4.1

The Nobel Peace Prize

Alfred Nobel became famous for two very different reasons. Nobel was first well-known for creating dynamite[1]. He created this important tool to make life easier for workers, and he made a lot of money from his **invention**. Unfortunately, people began to misuse[2] dynamite, and it caused great **suffering**. At the end of his life, Nobel worried that it would be the only reason people remembered him. As a result, he used most of his money to create an **organization** to give **prizes** to people who do the most good for the world. One of these was the Nobel Peace Prize. Nobel created this special prize for people who work the hardest to create peace in the world. Now, Nobel is perhaps even more famous for the Nobel Peace Prize than for dynamite.

[1]dynamite: an explosive
[2]misuse: to use something in the wrong way or for the wrong purpose

1. How is the simple past used in the paragraph?

    a. to write about a recent event

    b. to describe the events in a person's life

    c. to report on the result of an experiment

2. Why is the simple present used in the concluding sentence?

    a. to describe a habit

    b. to describe a fact

    c. to describe a process

Grammar: The Simple Past Affirmative

Simple past affirmative verbs end in *ed* or *d*.

SUBJECT	VERB	OTHER INFORMATION
I/You/He/She/It/We/They	**visited** **lived**	the university. in a small town.

For most verbs, add *ed* to make the simple past. However, when a verb ends:

• in *e*, add *d*. (live → lived)

• in a consonant + *y*, change the *y* to *i* and add *ed* (carry → carried)

Many verbs in English have an irregular simple past form. There is no rule that says when a verb is irregular, but you can look it up in a dictionary. Here are some common ones.

BASE	PAST	BASE	PAST	BASE	PAST	BASE	PAST	BASE	PAST
become	became	do	did	go	went	ride	rode	sit	sat
begin	began	eat	ate	have	had	run	ran	speak	spoke
buy	bought	feel	felt	leave	left	say	said	take	took
catch	caught	find	found	make	made	see	saw	teach	taught
come	came	get	got	pay	paid	send	sent	write	wrote

The verb *be* is irregular in the simple past. It has two forms.

SUBJECT	VERB	OTHER INFORMATION
I/He/She/It	**was**	at home.
You/We/They	**were**	excited.

For more information on the spelling of regular simple past verbs and a longer list of common irregular simple past verbs, see the *Writer's Handbook*.

ACTIVITY 2 | Identifying simple past verbs

Read the paragraph. Circle all the simple past verbs.

WORDS TO KNOW Paragraph 4.2

design: (v) to create
disappear: (v) to go away
improve: (v) to make better

machine: (n) equipment that uses power to do work
solve: (v) to find an answer or solution for something

PARAGRAPH 4.2

An Important Invention

Willis Carrier is not very well known, but he **designed** one of the most important inventions of the 20th century—the air conditioner. In 1902, Carrier worked as an engineer in a factory. A company in New York had problems with the air quality in its buildings, and Carrier wanted to help. He researched ideas to try to **solve** the problem. Not all his ideas worked, so he did more research. He **improved** his ideas and designed a **machine** as a solution to the problem. Finally, he wrote down all his notes and drawings and gave them to the company. The company built the machine and put it in its buildings, and the air problems **disappeared**. It took a long time for the air conditioner to become popular in family homes. However, now the whole world uses Carrier's invention even if they do not know who he was.

Air conditioning is essential at this indoor ski slope in Dubai, UAE.

ACTIVITY 3 | Using regular simple past verbs

Fill in each blank with the correct simple past form of the verb in parentheses.

> **WORDS TO KNOW** Paragraph 4.3
>
> **battery:** (n) a storage container for electricity
> **complicated:** (adj) difficult; complex
>
> **notice:** (v) to see
> **project:** (n) a specific task

PARAGRAPH 4.3

A Simple Solution

A university class **project** [1] _____ (help) two young women create a simple solution for a **complicated** problem. Julia Silverman and Jessica Matthews's professor at Harvard University [2] _____ (ask) the class to solve a world problem. Julia and Jessica [3] _____ (study) different countries with few energy sources. They [4] _____ (**notice**) that both adults and children in these countries [5] _____ (play) soccer every day. So Julia and Jessica [6] _____ (decide) to create a new energy source[1]. They [7] _____ (work) with friends to design a soccer ball with a **battery** in it. It took a long time, but they were finally successful. Julia and Jessica [8] _____ (name) their ball the SOCCKET and [9] _____ (show) it to users in El Salvador, Mexico, and South Africa. When players there [10] _____ (kick) the ball, the battery inside caught the energy from the ball's movement. After games, the players [11] _____ (use) the energy in the battery to power LED lights and cell phones, and they [12] _____ (love) it. It is amazing that a simple class assignment can improve the lives of so many!

[1]energy source: something that makes power for light, heat, etc.

Former US President Barack Obama plays with a SOCCKET.

ACTIVITY 4 | Using irregular simple past verbs

Fill in each blank with the correct simple past form of the verb in parentheses.

> **WORDS TO KNOW** Paragraph 4.4
>
> **achievement:** (n) a success   **hire:** (v) to pay someone to do a job
> **extraordinary:** (adj) unusual, uncommon

PARAGRAPH 4.4

Helen Keller (1880–1968)

Helen Keller lived quite an **extraordinary** life. When she
¹ _____ (be) two years old, she ² _____ (have)
a serious fever¹. It ³ _____ (make) her deaf and blind.
Because she could not hear or see, it was almost impossible for her to
communicate. When she ⁴ _____ (be) seven years old, her
parents **hired** Annie Sullivan to teach Helen. Although it was difficult at
first, Sullivan finally ⁵ _____ (teach) Helen to communicate
with sign language. This **achievement** opened a new world to Keller.
When Helen was 20 years old, she ⁶ _____ (begin) taking
college courses. After her graduation, she ⁷ _____ (write)
13 books and traveled around the world to talk about her life. Helen
Keller ⁸ _____ (be) an amazing person.

¹fever: a higher than normal body temperature, usually due to infection

Grammar: Past Time Words and Phrases

Past time words and phrases show when something happened in the past.

> last night   last week   the other day   this morning   (two minutes) ago   yesterday

You can put these expressions at the beginning or the end of a sentence. We often use a comma
after a time word or phrase at the beginning of a sentence.

    I watched the news **last night**.
    Last night, I watched the news.

ACTIVITY 5 | Writing sentences with irregular simple past verbs

Ask your partner the questions. Write each answer as a complete sentence.

1. Where were you last summer?

_____

2. How did you feel yesterday?

_____

3. What was the last funny movie you saw?

_____

4. What did you eat for lunch yesterday?

_____

5. Who did you send your last email to?

_____

Grammar: The Simple Past Negative

The negative simple past of all verbs, except *be*, is formed in the same way.

SUBJECT	DID + NOT + BASE FORM	OTHER INFORMATION
I/You/He/She/It/We/They	**did not arrive**	on time.

For the verb *be*, add the word *not* to make a negative sentence.

SUBJECT	BE + NOT	OTHER INFORMATION
I/He/She/It	**was not**	at the store yesterday.
You/We/They	**were not**	

Remember to:
- use *did not* + the base form of the verb

    ✓ Ahmed **did not** finish his homework.

    ✗ Ahmed did not finished his homework.

    ✗ Ahmed no finished his homework.

- use *was/were not* for the verb *be*

    ✓ Sandra **was not** in school yesterday.

    ✗ Sandra was no in school yesterday.

In informal writing, you can use the following contractions:

did not = didn't   was not = wasn't   were not = weren't

ACTIVITY 6 | Scrambled sentences

Unscramble the words and phrases to write correct sentences. Change the verbs to the negative simple past.

1. lived / in Singapore / three years ago / Carmen

Carmen did not live in Singapore three years ago.

2. Ling / engineering / last semester / studied

_____

3. last weekend / him / Humberto's parents / visited

_____

4. me / helped / Jack / with my presentation / yesterday

_____

5. Emma / an email / sent / this morning / to her parents

_____

6. with his academic advisor / spoke / Khaled / the other day

_____

7. I / my homework / yesterday / did

_____

8. the celebration early / Lan and Mei / last night / left

_____

9. went / my brother / last Saturday / to the grocery store

_____

10. on vacation / went / two days ago / Karla

_____

11. his customers / the other day / called / the salesman

_____

12. yesterday / in the cafeteria / had / my friends and I / lunch

_____

13. a long time / my drive to work / took / this morning

_____

14. a few days ago / a new lake / scientists / on Saturn / discovered

_____

ACTIVITY 7 | Using *be* in the simple past

Write the correct form of *be* in each blank. Use the negative form where indicated

Moving to the United States

My name is Panadda, and I ¹ _____ born in Thailand. I
² _____ (negative) the first child. My sister Suntri ³ _____
born three years before I ⁴ _____ born. My parents ⁵ _____
(negative) rich, but they ⁶ _____ always happy. They ⁷ _____
hard workers. In 2014, we moved to the United States. Everyone in my family
⁸ _____ very excited. We ⁹ _____ also scared. My mother
¹⁰ _____ (negative) able to speak English at all. When we arrived, she began
English classes. My sister and I started school. We ¹¹ _____ (negative)
comfortable in the classroom because we did not know the language. After a few years,
however, we learned the language and the culture of the United States.

A woman from Thailand becomes a U.S. citizen.

ACTIVITY 8 | Using the simple past

Write the simple past of the verbs in parentheses. Use the negative where indicated.

> **WORDS TO KNOW** Paragraph 4.6
>
> **be supposed to:** (phr) to be expected to   **horrible:** (adj) very bad; extremely unpleasant
> **crash:** (v) to fail suddenly   **yell:** (v) to shout

PARAGRAPH 4.6

Bob's Horrible Day

Bob ¹ _____ (have) a really **horrible** day yesterday. First, he
² _____ (be) **supposed to** get up at 6:00 a.m., but his alarm clock
³ _____ (work, negative). He ⁴ _____ (get up) at 8:00. There
⁵ _____ (be, negative) any hot water, so he had to take a cold shower. After
that, his car ⁶ _____ (start, negative), so he took the bus. When Bob ⁷
_____ (get) to work, his boss ⁸ _____ (**yell**) at him for being
late. Then his computer ⁹ _____ (**crash**), and he ¹⁰ _____
(lose) all of his work. He ¹¹ _____ (get, negative) home until midnight. He
¹² _____ (be) glad the horrible day was over.

ACTIVITY 9 | Writing sentences

The sentences below are false. With a partner, rewrite each using the negative form of the verb to make it true. You may use the Internet for help. Then write a true affirmative sentence.

1. John F. Kennedy was a leader in Mexico.

   John F. Kennedy was not a leader in Mexico. He was a leader in the United States.

2. Confucius lived in Colombia.

   _____

3. Ronaldinho played professional basketball.

   _____

4. Marie and Pierre Curie discovered penicillin.

   _____

5. The *Titanic* sank in the Pacific Ocean.

_____

6. Leonardo da Vinci came from Germany.

_____

7. Barack Obama was the president of Canada.

_____

8. J.K. Rowling wrote *Romeo and Juliet*.

_____

9. Steve Jobs created Microsoft.

_____

10. The 2018 FIFA World Cup took place in South Africa.

_____

ACTIVITY 10 | Writing a paragraph

On a separate piece of paper, write a paragraph about your family's past or about a difficult day you had. Include at least one compound sentence. Give your paragraph a title.

Grammar: Adverbs of Manner

Adverbs describe or give more information about verbs, adjectives, and other adverbs. Adverbs of manner usually describe verbs and end in *-ly*. They answer the question *How?*

> Kerry picked up the baby **carefully**.   (How did Kerry pick up the baby?)
>
> My sister is studying **hard**.   (How is my sister studying?)

Here are some common adverbs of manner.

badly	fast*	nervously	slowly
carefully	happily	quickly	suddenly
easily	hard*	quietly	well*

*These adverbs do not use the *-ly* form.

WRITER'S NOTE *-ly* Adjectives

Some words that end in *-ly* are adjectives, not adverbs.

deadly	friendly	lonely	lovely

ACTIVITY 11 | Using adverbs

Fill in each blank with an adverb that describes the underlined verb or verb phrase. Use an adverb from the list on page 93 or one of your own.

1. Julia <u>studied</u> _____ for the final exam. She was in the library every afternoon.

2. He <u>got onto</u> the bus _____ because it was raining.

3. Mariah <u>spoke</u> _____ at the conference. She was not used to speaking in front of so many people.

4. David <u>did</u> _____ in this class. He never studied.

5. Nili <u>cried</u> very _____ during the movie. I did not know she was crying until I looked at her.

6. Teresa <u>typed</u> her paper _____. She almost did not finish before class ended.

7. Nate <u>read</u> the directions _____. He did not want to make a mistake.

8. I had a cold, so I <u>did not play</u> _____ in the soccer game last week.

ACTIVITY 12 | Writing sentences with adverbs

Write original sentences using the adverbs given.

1. (easily)

_____

2. (happily)

_____

3. (suddenly)

_____

4. (hard)

_____

5. (quickly)

_____

6. (quietly)

_____

Grammar: Complex Sentences with Time Clauses

When you write, sentence variety will make your writing more interesting. Good writers use both simple and compound sentences.

> John played tennis. (simple sentence)
>
> John played tennis, and he was good at it. (compound sentence)

There is another way to add variety to your writing: **complex sentences**. A complex sentence consists of two clauses: an independent clause and a dependent clause. A clause is a group of words that includes a subject and a verb.

ind clause   *dep clause*
Joe listened to music after he watched TV. (complex sentence)

An independent clause can be a sentence by itself. A dependent clause cannot be a sentence by itself. It must be connected to the independent clause. If it is not, it is a fragment.

  ✓ **Before he bought a car,** John rode his bicycle to work.

  ✗ Before he bought a car. John rode his bicycle to work.

In a complex sentence, the dependent clause starts with a connector called a subordinating conjunction. Subordinating conjunctions such as *after*, *when*, *as soon as*, and *before* show the time order of events in a sentence. Dependent clauses that start with these time word connectors are called **time clauses**.

COMPLEX SENTENCES WITH TIME CLAUSES	
After + first action	**After** Leila finished school, she drove to work. Leila drove to work **after** she finished school.
When + first action	**When** my sister got sick, the doctor gave her some medicine. The doctor gave my sister some medicine **when** she got sick.
As soon as + first action	**As soon as** the group arrived in Portland, they toured the city. The group toured the city **as soon as** they arrived in Portland.
Before + second action	**Before** Josh took the driver's license exam, he practiced driving. Josh practiced driving **before** he took the driver's license exam.

For more information on connectors in complex sentences, see the *Writer's Handbook*.

Commas in Complex Sentences

When a complex sentence begins with the dependent clause, put a comma at the end of the clause. Do not use a comma when the dependent clause comes at the end of the sentence.

After she ate dinner, she called her friend.

She called her friend **after she ate dinner**.

ACTIVITY 13 | Identifying sentence types

Identify each sentence as *simple* (S), *compound* (CD), or *complex* (CX). If the sentence is compound or complex, add a comma when it is needed.

1. _____ Alexi and Juan finished their essays last night.

2. _____ Karl saw a movie this weekend but he thought it was really boring.

3. _____ Before Mahmood left class he spoke to the teacher about his homework.

4. _____ Amy expected to take a test today but she was wrong.

5. _____ The students did not have any questions after the teacher gave the assignment.

6. _____ My friends and I went down to the cafeteria and had lunch.

7. _____ We had enough time to get a coffee before class started.

8. _____ We can study here or we can go to the library.

9. _____ My brother flew to Amsterdam and he met our cousins there.

10. _____ When Karen wanted information for her report she went to the library.

11. _____ We cannot take a break before noon.

12. _____ The wildlife reserve protects elephants and their natural habitat.

13. _____ Sam began to study as soon as he got to the library.

14. _____ Ying asked a friend to edit her paper and she liked her friend's comments.

ACTIVITY 14 | Writing complex sentences

Combine the two simple sentences into a complex sentence using the connector in parentheses. Use pronouns when appropriate and the correct punctuation.

1. (as soon as)
First: I graduated from high school.
Second: I got a summer job.

As soon as I graduated from high school, I got a summer job.

2. (before)
First: Juan took some English classes.
Second: Juan traveled around the world.

3. (when)
First: My sister and I finished our homework.
Second: My sister and I went to a movie.

4. (after)
First: The house caught on fire.
Second: The fire department arrived very quickly.

5. (before)
First: The young woman looked left and right.
Second: The young woman crossed the street.

6. (when)
First: The lights in the classroom went out.
Second: The teacher told the students not to worry.

7. (as soon as)
First: Jacob had the freedom to study abroad.
Second: Jacob moved to California to study English.

BUILDING BETTER VOCABULARY

ACTIVITY 15 | Word associations

Circle the word or phrase that is more closely related to the bold word or phrase on the left.

1. be supposed to	have an accident	work hard
2. complicated	difficult	easy
3. crash	fail	save
4. disappear	come back	go away
5. extraordinary	usual	unusual
6. hire	get a job	give a job
7. horrible	extremely bad	extremely good
8. improve	your grades	your height
9. notice	ignore	see
10. suffering	pain	pleasure

ACTIVITY 16 | Collocations

Fill in the blank with the word that most naturally completes the phrase.

battery	organization	prize	project	solve

1. complete a _____ on time

2. join an _____

3. win a _____

4. _____ the mystery

5. recharge the _____

| achievement | design | hire | machine | yell |

6. _____ a new building

7. _____ at someone

8. _____ a new employee

9. a powerful _____

10. my greatest _____ in life

ACTIVITY 17 | Word forms

Complete each sentence with the correct word form. Use the correct form of the nouns and verbs.

NOUN	VERB	ADJECTIVE	SENTENCES
achievement	achieve		**1.** Her cancer research was her greatest professional _____ . **2.** I _____ a lot today.
improvement	improve	improved	**3.** Damon quickly _____ in his swimming classes when he was younger. **4.** This new computer software has many _____ .
invention	invent	inventive	**5.** The telephone was an important _____ . **6.** Some believe that Marconi _____ the radio, but others believe that Tesla created it.
suffering	suffer		**7.** The patient _____ from a rare disease. **8.** The medication greatly reduced the patient's _____ .
notice	notice	noticeable	**9.** The student _____ the mistake and corrected it. **10.** There are _____ differences among the cultures of the world.

ACTIVITY 18 | Vocabulary in writing

Choose five words from Words to Know. Write a complete sentence with each word.

1. _____
2. _____
3. _____
4. _____
5. _____

BUILDING BETTER SENTENCES

ACTIVITY 19 | Editing from teacher comments

Read the teacher's comments. Then make corrections.

> **PARAGRAPH 4.7**

Ibn Battuta

                                     capitalization   *verb tense*

Muhammad Ibn Battuta was a famous <u>moroccan</u> traveler. He <u>live</u> in Morocco in the

                missing verb   *verb tense*

14th century. When he_a young man, he made a trip to Mecca. Ibn Battuta <u>loves</u> to see new

                                   verb form   *punctuation*

places so much that he continued to travel. This <u>was no</u> his original plan_but he continued

                                    punctuation

on his journey. He had many adventures during his travels_and he met many interesting

                            verb form

people. After he returned home, he <u>did not forgot</u> about his journey. He wrote a book about

missing connector

his travels_this book now gives us a lot of important information about life in the 14th

     missing subject

century. Also,_gives us more information about this interesting and important man.

ACTIVITY 20 | Error correction

Find and correct the errors. The number in parentheses tells how many errors each sentence has.

1. We go to the park yesterday. (1)

2. The company president did not wrote the letter. (1)

3. Before he go home he finished his homework. (2)

4. The ice cream was delicious but the chocolate cake was better. (1)

5. We watched some of the movie but we leave early. (2)

6. Gary no graduated from college, but his sister finish in three years. (2)

7. Lauren weared her new dress, but she didn't liked it. (2)

8. After he was in the same job for five years his salary go up 25 percent. (2)

9. After the child ate his vegetables he ask for dessert. (2)

10. The baseball player catch the ball, but he drop it. (2)

ACTIVITY 21 | Combining sentences

Combine the ideas into one sentence. You may change the word forms, but do not change or omit any ideas. There may be more than one answer.

1. (HINT: Use a time connector.)
   Cassius Clay was 22 years old.
   At that time, he changed his name.
   His name changed to Muhammad Ali.

   _____

   _____

2. Valentina Tereshkova traveled to space.
   She did this before any other female astronaut.
   This happened on June 16, 1963.

   _____

   _____

3. (HINT: Use a time connector.)

Serena Williams was a young woman.

Serena Williams became famous for her tennis skills.

Her tennis skills were incredible.

_____

_____

WRITING

ACTIVITY 22 | Original writing practice

Think of an important historical event from the last one hundred years. Then follow these steps to write a paragraph about this event. Use the simple past, at least one complex sentence with a time clause, and at least two of the vocabulary words or phrases presented in the unit. Underline the unit vocabulary you use. Put a check (✓) next to each step as you complete it.

1. _____ In your first sentence, write the name of the event.

2. _____ In your next sentence, write where the event happened.

3. _____ In the next three or four sentences, explain what happened and why it was important.

4. _____ In the last sentence, summarize why this event was important.

Editing

After you finish your writing, check your work for errors. Use the checklist below to help you.

- ☐ I used the correct form of all simple past verbs.
- ☐ I used *after*, *when*, *as soon as*, or *before* to show time order in a complex sentence.
- ☐ I used commas correctly in complex sentences and with time words/phrases.
- ☐ Each sentence/clause has a subject and a verb.
- ☐ I included the four main parts of a paragraph and a title.

ACTIVITY 23 | Peer editing

Exchange papers from Activity 22 with a partner. Read your partner's paragraph. Then use Peer Editing Sheet 2 in the Writer's Handbook to help you comment on your partner's paragraph.

Additional Topics for Writing

Choose one or more of the topics to write about. Follow your teacher's directions.

TOPIC 1: Look at the photo on pages 82–83. A paleoanthropologist studies early humans. Do you think it is important to learn about the past? Why or why not?

TOPIC 2: Write about an event in the news last week. Who was involved? Where did it happen? Was it a good or a bad event? Explain.

TOPIC 3: Write about something funny that happened to you recently. What happened? Why was it funny?

TOPIC 4: Describe a place you visited when you were a child. Where was this place? Why did you go there? Who went with you? What did you do there?

TOPIC 5: Describe a time when you tried a new food. How old were you? Where were you? What did the food look (taste, feel, smell) like?

TEST PREP

You should spend about 25 minutes on this task. Write a paragraph with six to ten sentences.

Do you agree or disagree that progress is always good? Use specific reasons and examples to support your answer.

TIP

Pay careful attention to verb forms in your writing. Sometimes, you may use examples from the past to support your opinion about something in the present. When you do that, you need to switch between the simple past and the simple present.

Remember to use the simple past when you write about people, places, things, and events in the past. Use complex sentences with *after, when, as soon as,* and *before* to show time order.

5 | Writing about the Future

Arthur Huang is a National Geographic Emerging Explorer. He created the *Trashpresso*, a machine that turns plastic into building materials for walls and floors. He believes this is the future of recycling.

FREEWRITE Look at the photo and read the caption. Write about your experience with recycling. What types of things do you recycle? Do you own anything that is made from recycled materials?

ELEMENTS OF GREAT WRITING

Using *Be Going to* and *Will*

Be going to and *will* are used to talk about the **future**. They often have little or no difference in meaning. The future forms are less common in academic writing, but we use them to:

- make predictions (guesses about the future) and discuss expected results

  The community is going to/will benefit from the new park.
  The chemical is going to/will change the liquid to a bright blue color.

- talk about plans and proposals

  The president is going to/will meet with several world leaders on his trip.
  Many grocery stores are going to/will sell this new product.

ACTIVITY 1 | Analyzing sentences

Check (√) the use of *be going to* and *will* in each sentence.

	Prediction	Plan
1. Humans will live on Mars one day.	☐	☐
2. First, the scientists will research the problem.	☐	☐
3. That little boy is going to fall.	☐	☐
4. Arni is going to use two groups in his project.	☐	☐
5. The material will expand when it is in water.	☐	☐
6. The bear will be thin and hungry when spring arrives.	☐	☐
7. If you follow these steps, you will write a great research paper.	☐	☐
8. The team is going to use the information for their project.	☐	☐

Grammar: *Be Going to*

For some future meanings, we generally prefer one future form over the other. We use ***be going to*** for:

- future plans that are already made
- predictions that are based on a present action

SUBJECT	BE GOING TO		VERB (BASE FORM)
I	am		come to the party.
He/She/It	is	going to	travel next week.
			slip on the ice.
You/We/They	are		get wet from the rain.

SUBJECT	BE	NOT	GOING TO	VERB (BASE FORM)
I	am			come to the party.
He/She/It	is	not	going to	travel next week.
You/We/They	are			slip on the ice.
				get wet from the rain.

WRITER'S NOTE *Going to* vs. *Gonna*

Speakers of English often pronounce *going to* as *gonna*. However, do not use *gonna* in academic writing. You must write out the words completely.

✓ Our research is **going to** show that more studies are needed.

✗ Our research is gonna show that more studies are needed.

ACTIVITY 2 | Editing a paragraph

The paragraph has five errors with *be going to*. Find and correct them.

WORDS TO KNOW Paragraph 5.1

countryside: (n) land that is not in towns, cities, or industrial areas

sight: (n) a place to visit on a trip
spend: (v) to use time, money, etc.

PARAGRAPH 5.1

My Winter Vacation

My winter vacation going to be wonderful because I am going to go to Quebec. I am going to go there with my best friend. We going to **spend** one week in the city, and then we are going explore the **countryside** for a week. I have an aunt who lives there, and she is going to shows us all the beautiful **sights**. While I am there, I am going buy a lot of souvenirs[1] for my parents, brother, and friends. I cannot wait for my vacation to begin.

[1]souvenir: an object bought in order to remember a place

Quebec City, Canada, in winter

ACTIVITY 3 | Writing about the future with *be going to*

Answer the questions about Michael's schedule for next week. Write complete sentences with *be (not) going to.*

SUN	MON	TUES	WED	THURS	FRI	SAT
Eat lunch with Mom & Dad	Meet with Mr. Anderson Go running	Interview Andrew Pinter for the new job position	Finish business report for Ms. Simms Go for a bike ride	Take the day off of work Go to the doctor	Eat dinner with Bob Go running	Play soccer with friends

1. What is Michael going to do on Sunday?

   _____

2. Who is Michael going to interview on Tuesday?

   _____

3. On what day are Michael and Bob going to have dinner?

   _____

4. When is Michael going to meet with Mr. Anderson?

   _____

5. What are Michael and his friends going to do on Saturday?

   _____

6. What is Michael going to finish for Ms. Simms on Wednesday?

   _____

7. When is Michael going to go to the doctor?

   _____

8. What is Michael not going to do on Thursday?

   _____

9. On what days is Michael going to go running?

   _____

10. On what days is Michael not going to exercise?

   _____

ACTIVITY 4 | Making predictions

Work with a partner. Write as many predictions as you can about the image below. Write complete sentences using the correct form of *be going to*.

Guests have breakfast at Giraffe Manor in Nairobi, Kenya.

_____

_____

_____

_____

_____

_____

_____

_____

Grammar: *Will*

We generally use *will* for:

- future plans/decisions made in the moment
- strong predictions
- promises and offers to help

SUBJECT	WILL	VERB (BASE FORM)
I/You/He/She/It/We/They	will	answer the door. have a great time on vacation. help make dinner.

SUBJECT	WILL	NOT	VERB (BASE FORM)
I/You/He/She/It/We/They	will	not	drive to work in this snow. watch that boring movie. be late this time.

In informal writing, you can use these contractions:

I will = I'll	you will = you'll	he will = he'll	she will = she'll
it will = it'll	we will = we'll	they will = they'll	will not = won't

ACTIVITY 5 | Using *will*

Fill in each blank with *will* or *will not* and a verb from the box. You will use some verbs more than once.

be	buy	get	have	make	need

> **WORDS TO KNOW** Paragraph 5.2
>
> **advantage:** (n) a good part or feature
> **amount:** (n) a total, sum
> **disadvantage:** (n) a problem
>
> **mistake:** (n) an error
> **service:** (n) work paid for with money

PARAGRAPH 5.2

The Driverless Car Debate

When driverless cars become common, they [1]_____ both

advantages and **disadvantages**. One advantage will be fewer traffic accidents. Driverless cars

[2]_____ (negative) as many **mistakes** as humans because they

[3]_____ (negative) distracted[1]. Another advantage will be the

amount of time drivers have to do other things. They ⁴_____ able to use their time in the car to work, read books, watch TV, and so on. However, it is not clear how many people ⁵_____ a driverless car. Their high cost will be a disadvantage because many people ⁶_____ (negative) able to afford them. Another disadvantage will be fewer jobs. Taxi drivers and others in the transportation² business ⁷_____ less work because fewer and fewer people ⁸_____ their **services**. Whether good or bad, driverless cars will be here soon.

¹distracted: having one's attention pulled away
²transportation: ways to move from one place to another

A driverless shuttle in Las Vegas, USA

ACTIVITY 6 | Writing about the future with *will*

Make five predictions about what your life will be like in ten years. Use *will not* in at least one sentence.

1. _____

2. _____

3. _____

4. _____

5. _____

Grammar: Future Time Expressions

In Unit 1, you learned some common ways to express time. You can use many of the same expressions with *be going to* and *will*. Here are some other expressions you can use to show when something will happen in the future:

TIME WORDS AND PHRASES	PREPOSITIONAL PHRASES OF TIME
next Saturday/week/month/year	in a day/week/month/year
next time	in ten minutes/two hours
later	on the weekend/my birthday
tomorrow	by 2030

We often use a comma after time expressions when they are at the beginning of a sentence.

On Saturday, we are going to go to the movies.

We are going to go to the movies on Saturday.

Next year, the airline will use a new kind of jet.

The airline will use a new kind of jet next year.

ACTIVITY 7 | Identifying time expressions

Choose the correct word or phrase to complete the paragraph.

> **WORDS TO KNOW** Paragraph 5.3
>
> **hardly:** (adv) almost not
> **perform:** (v) to present or act in front of an audience
>
> **special:** (adj) important; meaningful

PARAGRAPH 5.3

Carmen's Fifteenth Birthday

[1](Later / Next) week, Carmen Viera will be 15 years old, and her family has plans for a **special** celebration for her. [2](In / On) her birthday, Carmen is going to wear a long white dress. [3](At / In) the morning, she is going to meet her family and friends. [4](At / On) noon, they will go to a ballroom[1] at a hotel. They are going to have a party there called a *quince*. When the party starts, Carmen will **perform** some formal dances with her friends. [5](Later / Next time), everyone is going to dance, eat, and celebrate. Carmen can **hardly** wait. She knows that she will always remember her special day.

[1]ballroom: a large room where important parties are held

Grammar: Complex Sentences about the Future

Remember that a complex sentence consists of an independent clause and a dependent clause. When the dependent clause begins with a time word connector, such as *after*, *when*, *before*, and *as soon as*, it is called a time clause. In a complex sentence about the future, use *be going to* or *will* in the independent clause, and use the simple present in the dependent (time) clause.

INDEPENDENT CLAUSE	TIME CLAUSE
Calvin **will take** a nap	<u>after</u> he **finishes** his work.
Maya **is going to read** a good book	<u>when</u> she **gets** home.
Those birds **will fly** south	<u>before</u> the weather **becomes** too cold.
Zainab **is going to make** a phone call	<u>as soon as</u> class **is** over.

Use a comma when the time clause is at the beginning of a sentence.

> **After he finishes his work,** Calvin will take a nap.

Remember to use the simple present in the time clause.

✓ Eliza will work on her painting **when she has time**.
✗ Eliza will work on her painting when she will have time.

Migrating Snow Geese in New Mexico, USA

ACTIVITY 8 | Choosing verbs for complex sentences in the future

Choose the correct form for each verb in parentheses.

> **WORDS TO KNOW** Paragraph 5.4
>
> **collect:** (v) to bring together
> **floating:** (adj) resting or moving on top of water or other liquid
>
> **garbage:** (n) trash
> **get rid of:** (phr) to throw away
> **recycle:** (v) to use again, especially waste items

PARAGRAPH 5.4

The Ocean Cleanup

Boyan Slat wants to **get rid of** the plastic **garbage** in our oceans. He started The Ocean Cleanup, an organization that is working on a safe and reliable way to do this. It is creating giant **floating** nets that will catch plastic near the top of the ocean but not harm any sea life. When the nets [1](are / will be) ready, the company [2](puts / will put) them into oceans near large areas of floating garbage. After the nets [3](are / will be) in place, the plastic garbage [4](flows / will flow) into them. When the nets [5](fill up / will fill up), large boats [6](**collect** / will collect) the garbage to **recycle** it. As soon as the newly recycled materials [7](are / will be) ready, they [8](go / will go) into a variety of products. The Ocean Cleanup estimates[1] that after it [9](uses / will use) its system for five years, the Giant Pacific Garbage Patch[2] [10](is / will be) fifty percent smaller. After it [11](cleans / will clean) that garbage patch, it [12](starts / will start) to clean up the other four garbage patches in the world. The oceans of the future will be cleaner places because of Boyan Slat and The Ocean Cleanup.

[1]estimate: to make a judgment about something
[2]Giant Pacific Garbage Patch: an area with a lot of trash in the Pacific Ocean between Hawaii and California, USA

Boyan Slat and his giant floating nets

ACTIVITY 9 | Writing complex sentences about the future

Combine the two simple sentences into a complex sentence about the future with the connector in parentheses. Use correct verb forms and punctuation.

1. (when)
First: A gardener adds fertilizer to a plant.
Second: The plant begins to grow.

_____

2. (as soon as)
First: The winter ice melts in the North Sea.
Second: Ships sail from port to port.

_____

3. (before)
First: I see how you drive.
Second: I lend you my car.

_____

4. (after)
First: The liquid heats up.
Second: The chemical reaction begins.

_____

5. (as soon as)
First: The air inside the balloon heats up.
Second: The air expands.

_____

6. (before)
First: The scientists discuss the project requirements.
Second: The scientists begin the work.

_____

7. (when)
First: I leave work.
Second: I call you.

_____

8. (after)
First: You choose your classes.
Second: You need to buy your books.

_____

Grammar: *If* Clauses

An ***if* clause** shows condition. As with time clauses about the future, we use *be going to* or *will* in the main clause and simple present in the dependent (*if*) clause.

INDEPENDENT CLAUSE	IF CLAUSE
We **are going to** be late	if we **do not leave** now.
You **will** do well on the test	if you **study** hard.
People **will** drive their cars less	if gas **becomes** very expensive.

Remember to use a comma when the *if* clause is at the beginning of a sentence.

If we do not leave now, we are going to be late.

ACTIVITY 10 | Using *if* clauses

Fill in each blank with the correct form of the verb in parentheses.

> **WORDS TO KNOW** Paragraph 5.5
>
> **benefit:** (n) a positive result   **tax:** (n) a necessary payment to the government
> **similar:** (adj) almost alike   **totally:** (adv) completely, entirely

PARAGRAPH 5.5

Philadelphia's Special Tax

People in Philadelphia, United States, have to pay a special **tax** now when they buy sweet drinks, such as soda. Officials believe that this will have several benefits. One advantage of the tax will be more government funding[1]. The city will use most of the money from the tax to improve its public schools, parks, recreation centers[2], and libraries. However, if people [1]_____ (buy) soda and other sugary drinks outside of the city, the government [2]_____ (not make) much money for these public services. Another advantage will be better health for the people of Philadelphia. Research on the subject shows that if people [3]_____ (have) to pay more for soda because of the tax, they [4]_____ (buy) less of it. Surprisingly, the same research shows that if people [5]_____ (want) to buy other types of sugary drinks, the tax [6]_____ (not change) their spending. For example, people continue to buy the same amounts of sweet tea and fruit juice in Philadelphia. Although the **benefits** of Philadelphia's tax on sugary drinks are not **totally** clear, several other cities in the United States now have a **similar** tax.

[1]government funding: money provided by the government to pay for something
[2]recreation center: a public building used for meetings, sports, activities, etc.

ACTIVITY 11 | Writing about the future with *if*

Write five sentences with *if* clauses that explain what will happen if you wake up late.

1. _____

2. _____

3. _____

4. _____

5. _____

Grammar: Reason Clauses

A **reason clause** answers the question *Why?* and often begins with the connector *because*. For reason clauses about the future, use *be going to* or *will* in the main clause. Use any appropriate verb form in the reason clause.

INDEPENDENT CLAUSE	REASON CLAUSE
They **are going to study** English	<u>because</u> they **want** to learn a second language.
I **will move** to Canada	<u>because</u> I **got** a job there.
Hanna **will work** from home tomorrow	<u>because</u> it **is going to snow**.

Remember that a reason clause is a dependent clause and cannot be a sentence by itself. If it is used by itself, it is a fragment.

✓ We are not going to go to the beach **because it is raining**.

✗ We are not going to go to the beach. Because it is raining.

Remember to use a comma when the reason clause is at the beginning of a sentence.

    Because they want to learn a second language, they are going to study English.

ACTIVITY 12 | Identifying sentences and fragments

Write S for *complete sentence* and F for *fragment*. Then add the correct capitalization and punctuation to the sentences.

1. ____S____ because he studies hard, Dante will do well in this class.

2. ____F____ because the weather will be bad on Saturday evening

3. _____ because it will be cold we are going to pack our heavy jackets

4. _____ because everyone had a wonderful time at the party

5. _____ because he is going to forget about his appointment

6. _____ because she is stuck in traffic she is going to arrive late

7. _____ because I live in New York City now I will go to the theater often

8. _____ because some students were not in class last week

9. _____ because the storm is really strong a lot of people will lose power

10. _____ because the managers are out of the office we are not going to have the meeting

ACTIVITY 13 | Writing complex sentences about the future

Complete each sentence with a reason clause.

1. Printed newspapers will not exist _____.

2. No one is going to use voicemail _____.

3. DVD players will disappear _____.

4. Classrooms are going to change _____.

5. Insects are going to be an important food source _____.

Lollipops with insects inside

ACTIVITY 14 | Combining sentences with *so* and *because*

Identify each sentence as *cause* (C) or *result* (R). Combine them into a compound sentence using *so*. Then combine them into a complex sentence using *because*. Use commas and subject and object pronouns as necessary.

1. a. _____C_____ I am thirsty.

b. _____R_____ I am going to drink a huge glass of water.

I am thirsty, so I am going to drink a huge glass of water.

I am going to drink a huge glass of water because I am thirsty.

2. a. _____ We are not going to play tennis.

b. _____ It is raining really hard.

_____

_____

3. a. _____ Mr. Lopez will take Ana to the doctor.

b. _____ Ana is very sick.

_____

_____

4. a. _____ I love the movie.

b. _____ I will recommend the movie to others.

_____

_____

5. a. _____ Jonathan does not feel well.

b. _____ Jonathan is not going to go to the party.

_____

_____

6. a. _____ I am not going to buy the new smartphone.

   b. _____ The new smartphone is very expensive.

_____

_____

7. a. _____ Brian will go to bed early.

   b. _____ Brian is extremely tired.

_____

_____

8. a. _____ Angela needs to buy some fruits and vegetables.

   b. _____ Angela is going to go shopping at the farmers' market.

_____

_____

ACTIVITY 15 | Review: Identifying sentence types

Identify each sentence as _simple_ (S), _compound_ (CD), or _complex_ (CX).

1. _____ I am going to go surfing next weekend.

2. _____ My father is going to retire next year, but my mother is going to keep working.

3. _____ After Gerardo finishes painting his house, it will look beautiful.

4. _____ Irene is going to call you when she gets home from work.

5. _____ Brett and his friends are going to go out for dinner and see a hockey game.

6. _____ Ariel is going to go to college next year, but her brother is going to get a job.

7. _____ The game is over, so we are going to go eat at Harvey's Grill.

8. _____ I will bring a salad and dessert to the party.

9. _____ Leslie and Serena will be roommates next semester, but they do not get along.

10. _____ If we do not finish this project on time, the company will lose the contract.

11. _____ Ana and her friends will not be able to go to the museum this weekend.

12. _____ We are going to visit our family in Mexico City because we have a long weekend.

ACTIVITY 16 | Review: Using commas

Combine the two sentences into one. Use the appropriate commas for compound sentences, complex sentences, and lists.

1. At the party, we ate food. We talked with our friends, and we played games.

_____

2. First, we are going to go to the store. Then we are going to make dinner.

_____

3. John wants to go to the movies. Rob and Theo want to go home.

_____

4. We will go to the Caribbean for our vacation. We will go to the beach every day.

_____

5. Elizabeth will not ride roller coasters. Roller coasters are too scary.

_____

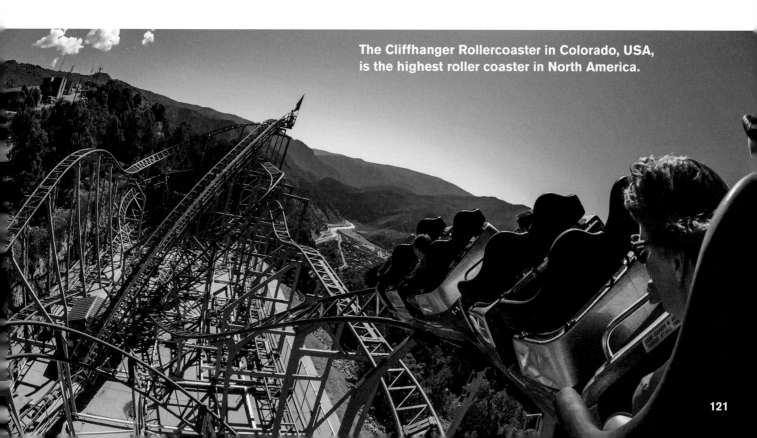

The Cliffhanger Rollercoaster in Colorado, USA, is the highest roller coaster in North America.

BUILDING BETTER VOCABULARY

WORDS TO KNOW

advantage (n)	disadvantage (n) AW	mistake (n)	similar (adj) AW
amount (n)	floating (adj)	perform (v)	special (adj)
benefit (n) AW	garbage (n)	recycle (v)	spend (v)
collect (v)	get rid of (phr)	service (n)	tax (n)
countryside (n)	hardly (adv)	sight (n)	totally (adv)

ACTIVITY 17 | Word associations

Circle the word or phrase that is more closely related to the bold word on the left.

1. advantage	benefit	weakness
2. collect	bring together	take apart
3. countryside	city	village
4. floating	on top of water	underwater
5. garbage	clean	dirty
6. mistake	error	solution
7. recycle	reuse	throw away
8. similar	different	same
9. spend	throw away	use
10. totally	barely	completely

ACTIVITY 18 | Collocations

Fill in the blank with the word or phrase that most naturally completes the phrase.

amount	disadvantage	get rid of	perform	special

1. _____ circumstances

2. _____ a song

3. a major _____

4. the _____ you need to pay

5. _____ whatever you do not want

hardly	mistake	recycle	sights	spend

6. _____ a few minutes on

7. do _____ any work at all

8. make a _____

9. _____ paper and plastic

10. see the _____

ACTIVITY 19 | Word forms

Complete each sentence with the correct word form. Use the correct form of the nouns and verbs.

NOUN	VERB	ADJECTIVE	SENTENCE PRACTICE
benefit	benefit	beneficial	**1.** There are many _____ to a good night's sleep. **2.** Speaking more than one language is _____ in today's economy.
collection	collect		**3.** Jennifer will come to your table and _____ your papers. **4.** My mother is going to sell her art _____.
mistake	mistake	mistaken	**5.** I thought that other person was you, but I was _____. **6.** We learn by making _____.
performance	perform		**7.** The teacher will grade our _____ on the test. **8.** The actors are going to _____ in a play next week.
tax	tax	taxable	**9.** Every employee must pay a _____ on the money they get from working. **10.** The money that waiters make from tips is _____.

ACTIVITY 20 | Vocabulary in writing

Choose five words from Words to Know. Write a complete sentence with each word.

1. _____

2. _____

3. _____

4. _____

5. _____

BUILDING BETTER SENTENCES

ACTIVITY 21 | Editing sentences

Find and correct the errors. The number in parentheses tells how many errors each sentence has.

1. If you are going to be at the beach you need to wear sunscreen. (1)

2. Everyone will bring their umbrellas, because it is going to rain. (1)

3. We are gonna meet them at the afternoon. (2)

4. The students going to go to the museum later. (1)

5. I am very hungry, because I will eat a big dinner tonight. (1)

6. They will type their ideas before they finished the project. (1)

7. When you spend time with my family, you will going to love them. (1)

8. The lights will turn on, as soon as you will push this button. (2)

9. The car is going to getting very hot if it is in the sun all day. (1)

10. After she makes the food, is going to take it to the table. (1)

11. Alison will go to the bookstore, so she needs books for her class. (2)

12. We will go shopping in Saturday. Because we need clothes for our vacation. (3)

ACTIVITY 22 | Writing about a photo

Write sentences about the photo. Use the connector in parentheses and *be going to* or *will*.

A crocodile swims close to photographer Jennifer Hayes.

1. (after)

_____

2. (when)

_____

3. (if)

_____

4. (because)

_____

ACTIVITY 23 | Combining sentences

Combine the ideas into one sentence. You may change the word forms, but do not change or omit any ideas. There may be more than one answer.

1. (HINT: Use an *if* clause.)
   We will go on a whale watch.
   We will do this next weekend.
   There must be good weather to do this.

_____

_____

2. (HINT: Use a reason clause.)
The runners will wear shirts.
The shirts are the same.
The reason is that they are a team.

_____

_____

3. (HINT: Use a time clause.)
First, Kevin will collect a lot of plastic bottles.
Second, Kevin will recycle the plastic bottles.

_____

_____

WRITING

ACTIVITY 24 | Writing a paragraph

Answer the questions. Then write a paragraph on a separate piece of paper. Try to use at least one time clause and one reason clause. Use at least two vocabulary words or phrases presented in the unit and underline them in your paragraph.

1. What is one important goal you have for the future? _____

2. When will you achieve this goal? _____

3. What three steps will you take to achieve the goal? Provide reasons for why these steps will help you.

   a. Step 1: _____

     Reason: _____

     _____

   b. Step 2: _____

     Reason: _____

     _____

   c. Step 3: _____

     Reason: _____

     _____

Editing

After you finish your writing, check your work. Use the checklist below to help you.

- ☐ I responded to all of the questions.
- ☐ I used *will* and *be going to* correctly.
- ☐ I used at least one time clause.
- ☐ I used reason clauses in my supporting sentences.
- ☐ I used commas correctly.
- ☐ I included the four main parts of a paragraph and a title.

ACTIVITY 25 | Peer editing

Exchange papers from Activity 24 with a partner. Read your partner's paragraph. Then use Peer Editing Form 2 in the *Writer's Handbook* to help you comment on your partner's paragraph.

Additional Topics for Writing

Choose one or more of the topics to write about. Follow your teacher's directions.

TOPIC 1: Review your Freewrite response for this unit. Think of all the ways that people recycle. Which types of recycling will have the biggest impact on the planet? Why?

TOPIC 2: Choose a current topic in the news. Read about it. Then write about what you think will happen and why.

TOPIC 3: Think about a special project or event that is going to happen in your neighborhood, city, or country. What is going to happen? When will it happen? Why is it going to happen? When will this project be complete?

TOPIC 4: Imagine that you are preparing to be away from home for a year. In addition to clothing and personal care items, what else will you take? Why?

TOPIC 5: Write about something that you plan to do in the next two weeks. Include the people who are going to be with you, what you are going to do, and why you are going to do this.

TEST PREP

You should spend about 25 minutes on this task. Write a paragraph with six to ten sentences.

What changes do you think will happen in this century? Give two specific examples and explain your choices.

Remember to use *be going to* and *will* to write about the future. Use time clauses, *if* clauses, and reason clauses to write complex sentences about the future. Pay attention to verb forms and commas in these complex sentences.

> **TIP**
>
> Avoid using words such as *always, never, all,* and *none.* You cannot give enough proof for these words. Instead, use words such as *probably, often, most, many, almost never,* and *almost none.*

6 | Sentence Variety

Students and parents outside of the Bonn International School in Germany, which has students from 78 different nations

OBJECTIVES
- Recognize sentence variety
- Write sentences with adjective clauses
- Use the modals *should*, *must*, *might*, and *can*
- Write an original paragraph

FREEWRITE | Look at the photo and read the caption. Write about some advantages of studying with people from different countries.

ELEMENTS OF GREAT WRITING

The Importance of Sentence Variety

Sentence variety is important in writing. Using compound and complex sentences in addition to simple sentences will make your paragraph more interesting.

Compare the following paragraphs. Both contain similar information about tennis terms. However, the paragraph in Example 2 reads better because there are a variety of sentence types.

EXAMPLE 1

Tennis Terms

Tennis has many special terms. They are used to discuss the game. Some people do not know the meaning of these special terms. They are not familiar with tennis. One special word is *love*. *Love* means "nothing" or "zero" in tennis. All tennis matches begin with a score of love-love. *Deuce* is a special word. It means the score is even. It means each player scored three points. This means the score is tied at 40. One other special term is *volley*. A *volley* means hitting the ball before it touches the ground. It comes from the French word *volée*. *Volée* means *flight*. *Love, deuce,* and *volley* are special terms. All tennis players and fans know these special terms.

Simple Sentences: 16   Compound Sentences: 0   Complex Sentences: 1

EXAMPLE 2

Tennis Terms

Tennis has many special terms that are used to discuss the game. Some people who are not familiar with tennis do not know the meaning of these special terms. One special word is *love*, and it means "nothing" or "zero" in tennis. All tennis matches begin with a score of love-love. *Deuce* is a special word that means the score is even. It means each player scored three points, so the score is tied at 40. One other special term is *volley*. A *volley* means hitting the ball before it touches the ground. It comes from the French word *volée*, and it means *flight*. *Love, deuce,* and *volley* are special terms that all tennis players and fans know.

Simple Sentences: 2   Compound Sentences: 3   Complex Sentences: 5

ACTIVITY 1 | Identifying sentence types

Look back at the paragraph in Example 2. Underline the simple sentences. Double underline the compound sentences. Notice the remaining complex sentences.

Grammar: Adjective Clauses

Adjective clauses are another way to add sentence variety to your writing. You can combine two simple sentences into a complex sentence with an adjective clause.

An adjective clause:

- has a subject and a verb
- describes a noun (just like an adjective does)
- often begins with *who* or *that*
- usually comes directly after the noun it describes

Notice how the two simple sentences are combined into a complex sentence with an adjective clause. The adjective clause is in bold. The noun it describes is underlined.

TWO SIMPLE SENTENCES	SENTENCE WITH AN ADJECTIVE CLAUSE
Tennis has many special terms. They are used to discuss the game.	Tennis has many special <u>terms</u> **that are used to discuss the game.**
Some people do not know the meaning of these special terms. They are not familiar with tennis.	Some <u>people</u> **who are not familiar with tennis** do not know the meaning of these special terms.
Deuce is a special word. It means the score is even.	Deuce is a special <u>word</u> **that means the score is even.**
Love, *deuce*, and *volley* are special terms. All tennis players and fans know these terms.	*Love*, *deuce*, and *volley* are special <u>terms</u> **that all tennis players and fans know.**

Who vs. *That*

When an adjective clause describes a person, use *who* or *that*.
When an adjective clause describes an animal, place or thing, use *that* (or *which*).

A tennis match in Monaco

ACTIVITY 2 | Identifying adjective clauses

The paragraph has five adjective clauses. Find and underline them. Then circle the noun or pronoun that is described by each adjective clause.

> **WORDS TO KNOW** Paragraph 6.1
>
> **consider:** (v) to think, believe
> **generation:** (n) a group of people of approximately the same age
>
> **grow up:** (phr v) to mature, become an adult
> **modern:** (adj) related to today's life
> **row:** (n) a line of things, people, etc.

PARAGRAPH 6.1

A Family Photo

This is a photo that shows the different **generations** and cultures in Ali Tecimen's family. Ali is the man in the blue jacket. He was born in Berlin, Germany. He **grew up** there, but his family is from Turkey. The two people in the front **row** are his grandmother and grandfather. They are the ones who brought the family to Berlin in the 1970s. They went there for work. Ali's parents are behind his grandmother. The young girl who is with them is Ali's daughter. The other woman in the photo is Ali's wife. The boy who is between them is their son. Even though Ali was born in Berlin and grew up there, he **considers** Turkey his home. This is a photo of Ali Tecimen's family, but it is also a picture that shows what many **modern** families look like.

Grammar: Subject Adjective Clauses

In **subject adjective clauses,** *who*, *that* or *which* is the subject of the verb.

TWO SIMPLE SENTENCES	SENTENCE WITH AN ADJECTIVE CLAUSE
Joe met a man. <u>The man</u> is very famous.	Joe met a man **who is famous**.
The subject is science. <u>This subject</u> was the hardest.	The subject **that was the hardest** was science.

ACTIVITY 3 | Using subject adjective clauses

Combine the two sentences into one. Change the second sentence into an adjective clause with *who* or *that* as the subject. The adjective clause should describe the noun in bold.

1. A coach is a **person**. This person trains athletes.

   A coach is a person who trains athletes.

2. Elon Musk is a **businessman**. He wants to make space travel easier and more common.

3. Romansch is a **language**. It comes from Latin.

4. Bolivia is a South American **country**. It does not have a coastline.

5. Nasi lemak is a Malaysian **dish**. It uses white rice and coconut milk.

6. Dante Alighieri was an Italian **poet**. He wrote *The Divine Comedy*.

7. A meerkat is an **animal**. It is a native of Africa.

8. The *Titanic* was a **ship**. It sank in the North Atlantic Ocean in 1912.

Grammar: Object Adjective Clauses

In object adjective clauses, *who*, *that*, or *which* is the object of the verb. In formal writing, *whom* is used instead of *who* or *that*.

TWO SIMPLE SENTENCES	SENTENCE WITH AN ADJECTIVE CLAUSE
They are meeting the teacher. Everyone <u>likes</u> _V the <u>teacher</u>. _O	They are meeting the teacher **who/whom/that** ^O everyone <u>likes</u>. _V
The girl is a new student. I <u>met</u> ^V <u>her</u> ^O in the hallway.	The girl **who/whom/that** ^O I <u>met</u> ^V in the hallway is a new student.

ACTIVITY 4 | Using object adjective clauses

Combine the two sentences into one. Change the second sentence into an adjective clause with *who*, *whom*, or *that* as the object. The adjective clause should describe the noun in bold.

1. The Guatemalan **dish** is called chilaquiles. I like this dish the best.

   The Guatemalan dish that I like the best is called chilaquiles.

2. The **movie** was *Black Panther*. We saw this movie at the theater last night.

3. The **dream** was strange. I had this dream last night.

4. The **number** was incorrect. Paul gave me this number.

5. The **story** was extremely interesting. Samir told this story.

6. The homework **assignment** was difficult. The grammar teacher gave us the homework assignment.

7. The **scientist** works in our lab. Many people admire this scientist.

8. The **food** got cold on our way home. We bought the food for dinner.

9. The famous **actress** was very friendly. I saw this actress at the restaurant.

10. The **play** is very popular in London. We are going to see this play tonight.

ACTIVITY 5 | Identifying adjective clauses

Underline the three sentences that have an adjective clause.

> **WORDS TO KNOW** Paragraph 6.2
>
> **complete:** (v) to finish something
> **encourage:** (v) to give strength or hope to someone
> **exist:** (v) to be present physically or emotionally
>
> **pay attention:** (phr) to observe and listen closely
> **the wild:** (n) an area away from people, towns, and cities

The National Geographic Photo Ark

There are many animals that are in danger of disappearing. Joel Sartore hopes to help save these endangered animals with the National Geographic Photo Ark. He plans to photograph the approximately[1] 12,000 animal species[2] that are in human care. These animals are in places such as zoos. He photographs animals in zoos because some species no longer **exist** in **the wild**. His pictures of these animals have black or white backgrounds that make people **pay attention** to each animal. The small, less popular animals look as important as the bigger, more well-known ones. It will take Sartore years to **complete** the Photo Ark, but he hopes his work will **encourage** people to care about the animals on our planet.

[1]approximately: close to a particular number or time
[2]species: a group of living things

A threatened koala with her babies

An endangered Florida panther

ACTIVITY 6 | Analyzing adjective clauses

Copy the three sentences that you underlined in Activity 5. Then write the simple sentences that were combined to make each complex sentence.

1. _____

_____

    a. _____

    b. _____

2. _____

_____

    a. _____

    b. _____

3. _____

_____

    a. _____

    b. _____

ACTIVITY 7 | Combining sentences

A. Combine the two sentences into one by using an adjective clause.

    1. This is the weather. I like this weather the most.

    _____

    2. People write _centre_ and _theatre_. These people use British English.

    _____

B. Sentence 1 belongs in Paragraph 6.3, and Sentence 2 belongs in Paragraph 6.4. Read the paragraphs and check (√) the best location for each sentence.

PARAGRAPH 6.3

How the Weather Affects Me

Some people do not believe the weather can change their **mood,** but it can really change mine. ☐ Rainy weather makes me feel **lazy**. It makes me want to stay inside and do nothing. I want to watch a movie or sleep. When the sun is **bright**, I feel energetic. ☐ This kind of weather makes me want to go outside. I want to play tennis or go to the beach. When the temperature is cool and the sun is shining, I feel like working. I want to finish my projects. As you can see, my mood **definitely** changes with the weather. ☐

PARAGRAPH 6.4

Spelling Differences

There are a few small but important spelling **differences** between British and American English. ☐ First, there is a difference in the use of *-re* and *-er* endings. ☐ However, these words are written as *center* and *theater* in American English. ☐ Second, British English has an **extra** letter to some words. For instance, *colour* and *travelling* in British English are *color* and *traveling* in American English. Finally, some words that end in *-ise* or *-ize* in British English can only be spelled *-ize* in American English. In British English, you can write *organise* or *organize*, but in American English you can only write *organize*. Although they are very similar, British and American English have some very different spelling rules.

Artist James Cochran (Jimmy C) works on his mural of William Shakespeare near the Globe theatre in London.

ACTIVITY 8 | Writing sentences with adjective clauses

Write a sentence with an adjective clause that describes each noun. Use the information in parentheses or your own ideas.

1. magazine (fashion articles) <u>I am reading a magazine that has many fashion articles.</u>

2. phone (good pictures) _____

3. teacher (a lot of homework) _____

4. animal (endangered) _____

5. invention (very important) _____

6. building _____

7. location _____

8. friend _____

9. university _____

10. gift _____

Grammar: Using Modals to Add Meaning

We use a **modal** before the base form of a verb to add meaning to that verb. Modals can be affirmative or negative. To make them negative, add *not*.

MODAL	PURPOSE	EXAMPLES
should (not)	to give advice	It is going to rain. You **should take** an umbrella.
must (not)	to show necessity	You **must have** a visa to visit that country.
might (not)	to show possibility	The weather is bad. We **might not go** to the beach.
can (cannot)	to show ability	Roberto **can speak** three languages.

We only use one modal before a verb.

✓ We **might** go to a new restaurant for dinner.

✗ We might can go to a new restaurant for dinner.

Remember to use the base form of the verb after the modal.

✓ We might **play** football tomorrow.

✗ We might to play football tomorrow.

ACTIVITY 9 | Choosing modals

Choose the modal that best completes each sentence. Sometimes both answers are possible.

> **WORDS TO KNOW** Paragraph 6.5
>
> **advice:** (n) an opinion about what to do   **skill:** (n) an ability to do something well
> **daily:** (adv) each day   **suggestion:** (n) a recommendation

PARAGRAPH 6.5

How to Improve Your English Quickly

Here is some good **advice** on how to improve your English quickly. First, you
[1](must / can) speak English as much as possible. This practice [2](can / must) help
improve your fluency[1]. Second, you [3](should / might) also make friends with
people who speak English well. This way, you [4](can / must) use your English more
often, and your new friends [5](can / must) help you by correcting your mistakes.
Third, you [6](should / might) read a lot in English. This will improve your
vocabulary. Finally, you [7](might / should) write in a journal **daily.** This [8](must / can)
help your writing **skills** improve quickly. These **suggestions** [9](should / must) help
your English get better faster.

[1]fluency: the ability to easily speak and write a language

ACTIVITY 10 | Using modals

You are preparing dinner for your friends. Answer the following questions with a modal.

1. What should you do before your friends arrive?

   _____

2. What must you do before dinner?

   _____

3. What can your friends do to help with the dinner?

   _____

4. What might you cook if there are twenty guests?

   _____

5. What should you do if one of the guests is late?

   _____

ACTIVITY 11 | Writing a paragraph

On a separate piece of paper, write a paragraph about things that someone should bring if they visit your country for a week. Explain why these things are necessary. Use modals.

ACTIVITY 12 | Identifying sentence types

Write S for *simple sentence*, CD for *compound sentence*, or CX for *complex sentence*. Then decide where each sentence belongs in Paragraph 6.6 and write its letter on the correct line.

a. _____ Okapis are actually in the same family as giraffes.

b. _____ Zebras and donkeys are part of the horse family, but they are different species.

c. _____ Zebras look like horses that have black and white stripes.

PARAGRAPH 6.6

Zebras, Donkeys, Horses, and Okapis

Zebras, donkeys, horses, and okapis have a lot of similarities. First, zebras and donkeys both look like horses. [1] _____ They are closer in size to donkeys though. Donkeys look like small horses with furry brown hair and long ears. [2] _____ Second, okapis look like a mix of a zebra and a donkey. They have legs that are striped like a zebra and a body that is dark brown like some donkeys. However, they are not part of the horse family. [3] _____ Although okapis, zebras, donkeys, and horses look alike, they are different.

A pair of okapis in a zoo

ACTIVITY 13 | Reviewing sequence words

Put the sentences in the correct order (1 through 9) to make a well-organized paragraph.

a. _____ While Victoria Falls, Iguazu Falls, and Niagara Falls all look different, they have several things in common.

b. _____ Additionally, Victoria Falls is on the border between Zambia and Zimbabwe.

c. _____ One way they compete is by having viewing platforms on each side of all the waterfalls.

d. _____ It is interesting to know how much these waterfalls have in common.

e. _____ For example, at least four major waterfalls come together to create Iguazu Falls.

f. _____ Finally, each waterfall is a major tourist attraction, and the countries compete with each other to get the most tourists.

g. _____ Next, each large waterfall is made up of smaller waterfalls.

h. _____ Iguazu Falls belongs to both Brazil and Argentina, and Niagara Falls is shared by Canada and the United States.

i. _____ First, each waterfall is owned by two countries.

BUILDING BETTER VOCABULARY

<table>
<tr><td colspan="4">WORDS TO KNOW</td></tr>
<tr><td>advice (n)</td><td>definitely (adv) AW</td><td>generation (n) AW</td><td>pay attention (phr)</td></tr>
<tr><td>bright (adj)</td><td>difference (n)</td><td>grow up (phr v)</td><td>row (n)</td></tr>
<tr><td>complete (v)</td><td>encourage (v)</td><td>lazy (adj)</td><td>skill (n)</td></tr>
<tr><td>consider (v)</td><td>exist (v)</td><td>modern (adj)</td><td>suggestion (n)</td></tr>
<tr><td>daily (adv)</td><td>extra (adj)</td><td>mood (n)</td><td>the wild (n)</td></tr>
</table>

ACTIVITY 14 | Word associations

Circle the word or phrase that is more closely related to the bold word or phrase on the left.

1. advice	command	opinion
2. bright	cloudy	sunny
3. complete	finish	start
4. consider	ignore	think about
5. daily	always	rarely
6. definitely	unsure	sure
7. exist	be somewhere	leave somewhere
8. grow up	become older	become larger
9. lazy	active	inactive
10. modern	old	new

ACTIVITY 15 | Collocations

Fill in the blank with the word or phrase that most naturally completes the phrase.

grow up	mood	row	suggestion	the wild

1. sit in the front _____

2. make a _____

3. _____ in a small town

4. be in a bad _____

5. live in _____

| difference | encourage | generation | pay attention | skill |

6. develop a _____

7. _____ to the directions

8. the next _____

9. there is no _____

10. _____ someone to continue

ACTIVITY 16 | Word forms

Complete each sentence with the correct word form. Use the correct form of the nouns and verbs.

NOUN	VERB	ADJECTIVE	SENTENCE PRACTICE
advice	advise		**1.** When I have a problem, my mother always gives me good _____ . **2.** My college counselor _____ me to take geometry last semester.
difference	differ	different	**3.** What's the _____ between your new laptop and your old one? **4.** My generation _____ from my parents' generation in many ways.
encouragement	encourage	encouraging	**5.** Teachers usually offer a lot of _____ to their students. **6.** My friend _____ me to travel.
	modernize	modern	**7.** The government will _____ its office buildings next year. **8.** _____ technology is amazing.
suggestion	suggest		**9.** The city wants the citizens to _____ ideas for the new park. **10.** Cindy's _____ will help our project.

ACTIVITY 17 | Vocabulary in writing

Choose five words from Words to Know. Write a complete sentence with each word.

1. _____

2. _____

3. _____

4. _____

5. _____

BUILDING BETTER SENTENCES

ACTIVITY 18 | Editing a paragraph

The paragraph has eight errors. Find and correct them.

1 adjective clause error	2 comma errors	1 compound sentence error
2 capitalization errors	1 word order error	1 possessive adjective error

PARAGRAPH 6.7

Visiting a New Country

There are many reasons to visit a new country. First, you can see beautiful interesting and distant places. For example, you can visit the Kremlin and Red Square in russia. Another reason to travel is to eat new types of food. If you visit Thailand, you can drink jasmine tea, you can eat coconut-flavored rice. Finally, you can meet new people which live in these different places. you can talk to people and learn more about his likes and dislikes. As you can see, traveling to another country is important for reasons different.

The Kremlin in Moscow, Russia

ACTIVITY 19 | Scrambled sentences

Each of the scrambled sentences is missing one word. Unscramble the words and phrases. Then add the missing word to write a correct sentence.

1. in Hawaii / every year / go / to our beach house

We go to our beach house in Hawaii every year.

2. Kevin / at the dentist's office / an appointment / at 4:30 p.m.

3. got / a nice gift / James / last week / for birthday

4. eats lunch and talks / to her friends / every day / Suri / the cafeteria

5. works / Mary / every day / hard / a new car / wants to buy / because

6. Mount Erebus / a volcano / has / a lava lake / is

ACTIVITY 20 | Combining sentences

Combine the ideas into one sentence. You may change the word forms, but do not change or omit any ideas. There may be more than one answer.

1. The two women are my grandmother and mother.
The women are on the porch.

2. Parents often give advice.
They want their children to take this advice.

3. Archaeologists must get permission from landowners.
These archaeologists want to explore private land.

WRITING

ACTIVITY 21 | Writing a paragraph

Write a paragraph on a separate piece of paper on the following topic:

> *On the weekends, do you prefer to cook and eat at home or eat in a restaurant? Why?*

Follow these steps for writing. Put a check (✓) next to each step as you complete it. Additionally, include at least one adjective clause, one compound sentence, two modals, and two vocabulary words or phrases presented in the unit in your paragraph. Underline the vocabulary.

1. _____ In your first sentence, tell which dining choice you prefer.

2. _____ In the supporting sentences, give two or three reasons why you prefer this type of experience.

3. _____ Give details for each of your reasons.

4. _____ In the last sentence, summarize your opinion about the experience that you prefer.

Editing

After you finish your writing, check your work for mistakes. Use the checklist below to help you.

- ☐ I gave my opinion in the first sentence.
- ☐ I gave two or three reasons in my supporting sentences.
- ☐ I gave details for each of my reasons.
- ☐ I summarized my opinion in the last sentence.
- ☐ I used at least one adjective clause.
- ☐ I used at least one compound sentence.
- ☐ I used commas correctly in compound and complex sentences.
- ☐ I used at least two modals.
- ☐ I used at least two vocabulary words or phrases from the unit and underlined them.
- ☐ I included the four main parts of a paragraph and a title.

ACTIVITY 22 | Peer editing

Exchange papers from Activity 21 with a partner. Read your partner's paragraph. Then use Peer Editing Form 2 in the *Writer's Handbook* to help you comment on your partner's paragraph.

Additional Topics for Writing

Choose one or more of the topics to write about. Follow your teacher's directions.

TOPIC 1: Describe your class. How many students are in it? Where are you all from? How are you similar? How are you different?

TOPIC 2: Write about your dream house or apartment. Describe what this house looks like (its size, style, color, etc.). Write about the location of the house (in the mountains, on the beach, in a big city, etc.).

TOPIC 3: Write about an important discovery. What is it? Why is it important? Why do you find this discovery so interesting?

TOPIC 4: Describe a painting that you like. Who painted it? What is in the painting? Describe the colors. What do you feel when you look at the painting?

TOPIC 5: Describe your favorite kind of shopping. Where do you shop? What do you shop for? What do you like about the experience?

TEST PREP

You should spend about 25 minutes on this task. Write a paragraph with six to ten sentences.

Some universities require students to take classes in many subjects. Other universities require students to specialize in one subject. Which is better? Use specific reasons and examples to support your answer.

> **TIP**
>
> It is important to show sentence variety in your writing. A simple sentence is more meaningful if you use it along with compound and complex sentences. When your writing is varied, it sounds stronger and more academic.

Remember to use adjective clauses to describe nouns to add variety to your sentences. Use the modals *should*, *must*, *might*, and *can* to express advice, necessity, possibility, and ability.

7 | Reader Response

OBJECTIVES
- Use sequence words to organize ideas
- Express an opinion using an opinion verb + *that* clause
- Write a response paragraph
- Write an original paragraph

Two men have a conversation near the Brooklyn Bridge in New York City, USA.

FREEWRITE | Look at the photo and read the caption. Write about conversations you have with your friends. What do you talk to them about? Do you ever disagree? Explain.

ELEMENTS OF GREAT WRITING

Listing

Writers often organize their ideas in **lists**: by number, time, or importance. A topic sentence for a paragraph with listing order often includes a phrase such as *many types*, *several reasons*, *three steps*, etc.

> There are **several reasons** for the recent increase in sales.
> All new students must go through **four steps** before they can register for classes online.

In this kind of paragraph, it is important to signal the order of ideas with sequence words and phrases. Here are some common sequence words and phrases for listing.

First/Second/Third	Last	A/An/One (reason/example)
Next	Finally	Another (reason/example)
Then	The first/next/last (reason/example)	In addition

First, *next*, *then*, *last*, *finally*, and *in addition* are adverbs and often come at the beginning of a sentence followed by a comma (except for *then*).

> **First,** passengers buy a ticket.
> **Next,** they go through the gate.
> **Then** they wait for the train.

With *one (reason/example)*, *the next (reason/example)*, and *another (reason/example)*, do not use a comma.

> **The next reason** to read is to increase your vocabulary.
> Barcelona **is another example** of a city with unusual buildings.

ACTIVITY 1 | Identifying topic sentences for listing paragraphs

Check (√) the topic sentences for paragraphs with listing order.

1. _____ There are three major oceans on Earth.

2. _____ To make good sushi, chefs follow specific steps.

3. _____ Soccer is the most popular sport in the world.

4. _____ Students take online classes for several reasons.

5. _____ The biggest reason for climate change is human activity.

6. _____ Although reading online is convenient, it is difficult to read deeply.

7. _____ The U.S. government is divided into three branches.

8. _____ The water cycle has four stages.

9. _____ Parents should allow children more freedom.

10. _____ Skydiving seems extremely dangerous, but it is actually quite safe.

ACTIVITY 2 | Choosing sequence words

Fill in each blank with the correct sequence word or phrase. Use correct capitalization.

a second	another	finally	first	in addition

> **WORDS TO KNOW** Paragraph 7.1
>
> **access:** (v) to get into something; enter
> **effect:** (n) a result
> **issue:** (n) a topic or matter of concern
>
> **natural:** (adj) formed by nature; not man-made
> **produce:** (v) to make, create
> **trend:** (n) a current style or pattern

PARAGRAPH 7.1

Trends in City Design

Five **trends** are changing the way we design cities. [1]_____, we are paying more attention to people and their needs. As a result, residents are much closer to shopping and restaurants that they love. It is also easier for them to **access** public transportation and use bike paths. [2]_____ trend is creating healthier buildings. These buildings have more **natural** light and fewer chemicals. Bringing more nature into cities is [3]_____ trend. We can see this in cities that have green spaces and tree-planting programs. [4]_____, we are thinking about the **effects** of climate change[1]. Bad storms, flooding, and rising sea levels are just a few **issues** we need to consider when designing cities. [5]_____, there is a trend toward sustainability. More and more buildings are **producing** their own energy. As we change, our cities change, too.

[1]climate change: changes in Earth's weather patterns

A green space on top of Namba Parks shopping complex in Osaka, Japan

151

Mayon Volcano on Luzon Island, in the Philippines

ACTIVITY 3 | Organizing a paragraph

Put the sentences in paragraph order (1–8). Use the sequence words to help you.

a. _____ The Philippines faces a number of dangers related to weather.

b. _____ Finally, the Philippines is located on the Pacific Ring of Fire.

c. _____ These warm temperatures cause major storms called typhoons to develop.

d. _____ The Ring of Fire is an area that has a lot of earthquakes and volcanoes.

e. _____ Second, the heavy rain from storms can cause mudslides.

f. _____ These reasons explain why the Philippines experiences extreme weather.

g. _____ First, the Philippines is by the equator, so water temperatures are very warm.

h. _____ Mudslides are becoming a big problem because so many of the forests on the islands were cut down.

Responding to Ideas

Students in academic classes often need to respond to or give their opinion about something they read, watch, or discuss. A **response paragraph** is usually about a topic that people have strong opinions about. There are typically three types of responses: agree, disagree, and a mix of both.

A response paragraph should have:

- a topic sentence that states your opinion
- supporting sentences that give reasons and examples to support your opinion
- a concluding sentence that summarizes your opinion or offers a suggestion

ACTIVITY 4 | Analyzing a response

Read Paragraph 7.2. Then read the response in Paragraph 7.3 and answer the questions that follow.

WORDS TO KNOW Paragraphs 7.2 to 7.3

argue: (v) to fight with words
continue: (v) to carry on for a period of time
development: (n) growth or progress
focus: (v) to center one's attention on
join: (v) to become a member of a group

necessary: (adj) required, needed
opportunity: (n) a chance, possibility
provide: (v) to supply
reduce: (v) to make something smaller, decrease

PARAGRAPH 7.2

Reducing Time for Physical Education

Many U.S. elementary and high schools are **reducing** the time students have for physical education during the school day. They are doing this to give students more time to **focus** on academic work and to invest[1] in more academic subjects. People who agree with this action say students need to spend more time preparing for national tests. In addition, they **argue** that not all students like to take physical education classes. They say that students who like exercise can **join** an afterschool sports program. However, people who disagree with this action say that not all students can access activities outside of school. They also argue that exercise is **necessary** for young people's brains as well as their bodies. They mention that brain **development** is connected to exercise and can help students do better in their academic classes. Despite the debate[2], students **continue** to lose their physical education classes.

[1]invest: to put effort or money into something
[2]debate: an argument; discussion

A gym class in
Colorado, USA

More Attention to Education

I believe that schools should focus on education, not exercise, for three reasons. One reason is that they need to give students more **opportunities** to get academic information. **Providing** time for gym class takes away these opportunities. In addition, students need more time to prepare for national tests, such as college entrance exams. They should practice test-taking skills, not sports. Finally, students need to be able to compete academically in college. They will be at a disadvantage if the other students in their classes studied more than they did in elementary and high school. For these reasons, I believe a school's job is to educate minds, not exercise bodies.

1. What is the writer's opinion? _____

2. What three reasons does the writer include?

    a. _____

    b. _____

    c. _____

3. Is the concluding sentence a summary or a suggestion? _____

Grammar: Opinion Verbs + *That* Clauses

To express an opinion, you can use an opinion verb + *that* clause. A ***that* clause** (also called a noun clause) is a dependent clause that contains a subject, verb, and possibly other information. It answers the question *What?*

OPINION VERB	THAT CLAUSE: S + V (+ OTHER INFORMATION)
I **believe**	**that** <u>students</u> should <u>have</u> school on Saturdays.
I **feel**	**that** <u>having pets</u> <u>teaches</u> children about responsibility.
I **think**	**that** <u>people</u> <u>should be</u> able to vote at 16.
I **agree**	**that** <u>helping others</u> <u>is</u> important.
I **disagree**	**that** <u>video games</u> <u>make</u> players violent.

Note that we can use the modal *should* to make a suggestion.

    We **should** start a tree-planting program in our city.

ACTIVITY 5 | Analyzing a response paragraph

Read another response to Paragraph 7.2. Underline all the *that* clauses. Then answer the questions that follow.

> **WORDS TO KNOW** Paragraph 7.4
>
> **chance:** (n) an opportunity **unfair:** (adj) not fair or just
> **habit:** (n) a repeated behavior; routine

PARAGRAPH 7.4

Keep Physical Education

There are several reasons why I do not think that schools should reduce the time for physical education. First, I think that it is **unfair** to make students sit in class all day. They need a **chance** to take a break and move around. Second, exercise brings oxygen to our brains. This can help students focus better on their lessons and learn more. Last, I believe that physical education classes teach students healthy **habits**. This is important because students will miss fewer classes if they are healthy. I truly feel that reducing the time for physical education in schools is not a good idea.

A physical education class in Bahrain

1. What is the writer's opinion? _____

2. What three reasons does the writer include?

   a. _____

   b. _____

   c. _____

3. Is the concluding sentence a summary or a suggestion? _____

ACTIVITY 6 | Using *that* clauses

The paragraph is missing the three *that* clauses below. Decide where each belongs and write it on the line. Then answer the questions that follow.

that exercise has a place in schools

that schools should focus on academics

that schools should find different ways to get students to exercise

---

WORDS TO KNOW Paragraph 7.5

compromise: (n) an agreement reached where each side gets some but not all of what it wants

lack: (n) not enough of something

PARAGRAPH 7.5

Academics and Exercise

I have mixed feelings about the **lack** of physical education in schools. On the one hand,

I agree ¹ _____.

If students are more educated, they will be more competitive in college and at work. On the

other hand, I believe ² _____

_____. If students are in poor physical health, it is hard

for them to learn. I think ³_____

_____. They should find a **compromise**.

---

1. What is the writer's opinion? _____

2. What two reasons does the writer include?

    a. _____

    b. _____

3. Is the concluding sentence a summary or a suggestion? _____

ACTIVITY 7 | Writing sentences

A. Write a sentence with your opinion about each topic. Use an opinion verb + *that* clause.

1. animals in zoos

_____

2. children watching TV

_____

3. social media

_____

4. going on a diet

_____

5. taking a year off before going to college

_____

6. telling a lie to be polite

_____

7. requiring shoppers to use their own bags

_____

8. driverless cars

_____

B. Choose two of your opinions. Write them on the lines below and list three reasons for each one. Then share your ideas with a partner.

Opinion 1: _____

    Reason a: _____

    Reason b: _____

    Reason c: _____

Opinion 2: _____

    Reason a: _____

    Reason b: _____

    Reason c: _____

BUILDING BETTER VOCABULARY

WORDS TO KNOW

access (v) **AW**	development (n)	join (v)	produce (v)
argue (v)	effect (n)	lack (n)	provide (v)
chance (n)	focus (v) **AW**	natural (adj)	reduce (v)
compromise (n)	habit (n)	necessary (adj)	trend (n) **AW**
continue (v)	issue (n) **AW**	opportunity (n)	unfair (adj)

ACTIVITY 8 | Word associations

Circle the word or phrase that is more closely related to the bold word on the left.

1.	**argue**	disagree	agree
2.	**chance**	possibility	example
3.	**continue**	stop	go
4.	**focus**	confusion	attention
5.	**issue**	topic	answer
6.	**necessary**	extra	required
7.	**produce**	break	make
8.	**provide**	give	take
9.	**reduce**	bigger	smaller
10.	**unfair**	equal	unequal

ACTIVITY 9 | Collocations

Fill in the blank with the word or phrase that most naturally completes the phrase.

access	compromise	development	habit	lack

1. have a bad _____

2. reach a _____

3. _____ the building

4. canceled due to a _____ of interest

5. physical _____

| focus | natural | necessary | opportunity | trend |

6. an excellent career _____

7. start a _____

8. be _____ for growth

9. _____ on your studies

10. made out of _____ materials

ACTIVITY 10 | Word forms

Complete each sentence with the correct word form. Use the correct form of the nouns and verbs.

NOUN	VERB	ADJECTIVE	SENTENCE PRACTICE
access	access	accessible	**1.** Students do not have _____ to the building at night. **2.** The university is _____ by bus, train, and subway.
development	develop	developed	**3.** A storm _____ over the ocean yesterday. **4.** Social _____ is important for young children.
product	produce	productive	**5.** Writing a list of things to do helps some people to be more _____ . **6.** Coffee is a _____ of Brazil.
provision	provide		**7.** The company _____ cars to employees when they travel. **8.** The Red Cross is in charge of the _____ of food and water after a disaster.
reduction	reduce	reduced	**9.** The _____ in sales means the company has to close three offices. **10.** To lose weight, people need to _____ the amount of food they eat and increase their exercise.

ACTIVITY 11 | Vocabulary in writing

Choose five words from Words to Know. Write a complete sentence with each word.

1. _____

2. _____

3. _____

4. _____

5. _____

BUILDING BETTER SENTENCES

ACTIVITY 12 | Identifying errors

Find and correct the errors. The number in parentheses tells how many errors each sentence has.

1. I think that children should has more free time. (1)

2. Addition, they should watch less TV. (1)

3. And final, children need to play outside. (1)

4. Better health is another reasons to join a gym. (1)

5. An example of famous painting is the *Mona Lisa*. (1)

6. More people is going to live longer because of his healthier habits. (2)

7. He disagrees that parents should to help children with homework. (1)

8. They believes that everyone have a talent or can do something special. (2)

9. The last examples of a coffee producer are Brazil. (2)

10. We feel that planning for the future are important. (1)

ACTIVITY 13 | Writing sentences

Write an original sentence using the words listed.

1. (weather/hurricane)

_____

2. (TV/reason)

_____

3. (example/fun activity)

_____

4. (disagree/necessary)

_____

5. (reduce/unfair)

_____

6. (trend/continue)

_____

7. (issue/focus on)

_____

8. (opportunity/provide)

_____

ACTIVITY 14 | Combining sentences

Combine the ideas into one sentence. You may change the word forms, but do not change or omit any ideas. There may be more than one answer.

1. Some cars are electric.
They are better for the environment.
I believe that.

_____

_____

2. There are many beaches near my house.
These beaches are popular places to go.
They are popular in the summer.

_____

_____

3. Jenna likes to travel alone.
She meets people.
She can do what she wants.

WRITING

ACTIVITY 15 | Writing a paragraph

Read Paragraph 7.6. Then follow the steps below to write a response paragraph on a separate piece of paper. Use at least two vocabulary words or phrases presented in the unit and underline them in your paragraph.

A man sets a clock in Minsk, Belarus.

PARAGRAPH 7.6

Changing the Clocks

In many countries, people change the time on their clocks twice a year in a practice called daylight saving time. People who support daylight saving time say that more light in the evening means we use lights and electricity less. However, because we use a lot of our power for heat and air conditioning, this change in daylight hours does not help us save much energy. In the beginning, supporters argued that the time change helped farmers because they could work longer into the evening during the summer. But this change in schedule can be very hard on our bodies as it makes people more tired and even causes heart attacks to increase. One argument for daylight saving time continues to be strong—people spend more money on evening activities, so businesses do well. In addition, some types of crime decrease because of more light in the evening. Although this practice is becoming less popular, it still continues in many places.

1. _____ State your opinion in your topic sentence. Use an opinion verb + *that* clause.

2. _____ Give several reasons or examples to support your opinion.

3. _____ Use sequence words and phrases to organize the ideas in your supporting sentences.

4. _____ In your concluding sentence, summarize your opinion or offer a suggestion.

5. _____ Give your paragraph a title.

Editing

After you finish your writing, check your work for mistakes. Use the checklist below to help you.

- ☐ I wrote a topic sentence that states my opinion and is indented.
- ☐ I wrote a sufficient number of supporting sentences related to the topic.
- ☐ I used sequence words and phrases to organize my ideas.
- ☐ I wrote a concluding sentence that summarizes my opinion or offers a suggestion.
- ☐ I gave my paragraph a title.

ACTIVITY 16 | Peer editing

Exchange papers from Activity 15 with a partner. Read your partner's paragraph. Then use Peer Editing Form 2 in the *Writer's Handbook* to help you comment on your partner's paragraph.

Additional Topics for Writing

Choose one or more of the topics to write about. Follow your teacher's directions.

TOPIC 1: Do you think an online class is as good as a traditional class? Why or why not?

TOPIC 2: Do you think that reality TV programs are beneficial? Why or why not?

TOPIC 3: Do you think that babies and young children should be allowed to use smart phones or tablets? Why or why not?

TOPIC 4: Some parents schedule a lot of activities for their children outside of school. Do you think this is a good idea? Why or why not?

TOPIC 5: Do you think that art classes are important in education? Why or why not?

TEST PREP

You should spend about 25 minutes on this task. Write a paragraph with six to ten sentences.

Some people think that playing games is a waste of time. Other people think that games teach valuable life lessons. Which opinion do you agree with? Use specific reasons and details to support your answer.

> **TIP**
>
> It is generally easier either to agree or disagree only in your response, rather than a mix of both. If you have ideas for both sides, choose the side that is easier for you to write about. If you do not have a strong opinion, choose the side you can write about best—you receive points for your writing skill, not your true personal beliefs. Once you pick a side, only write ideas that support that side.

Remember to use sequence words and phrases to help organize your ideas. Use an opinion verb + *that* clause to express your opinion.

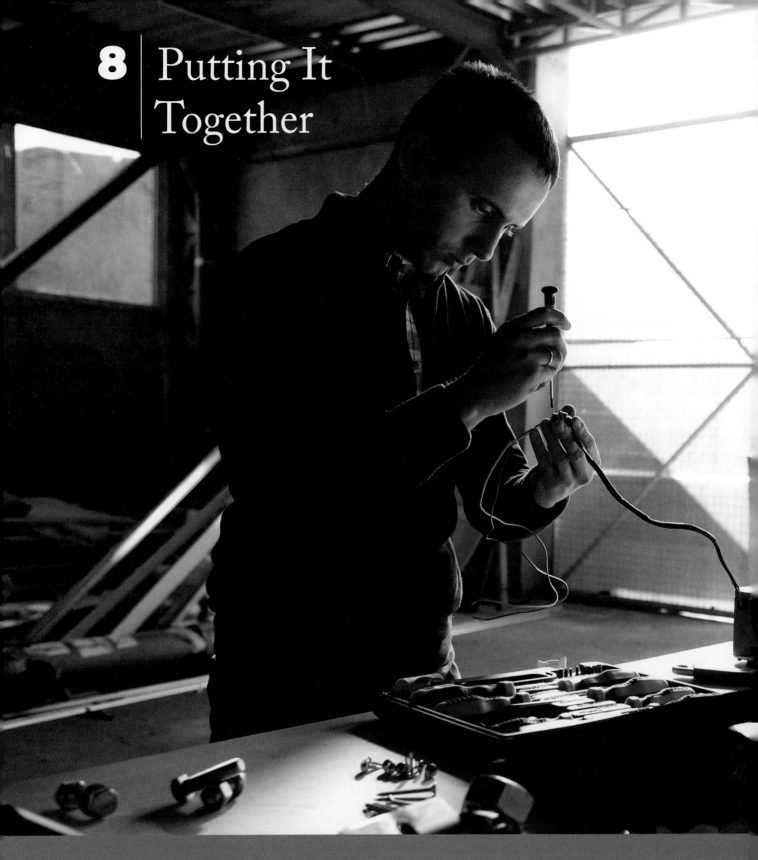

8 | Putting It Together

OBJECTIVES
- Review paragraph basics
- Write an original paragraph
- Edit your paragraph for grammar and sentence variety

Bosnian inventor Elvis Cero works on part of his electric folding car.

FREEWRITE | Look at the photo and read the caption. What is something that you put together recently? Write about the important steps of that process.

ELEMENTS OF GREAT WRITING

Reviewing Paragraph Basics

When you write a **paragraph**, remember to:

- **indent** the first line
- include a **topic sentence** that states the main idea
- develop the main idea with **supporting sentences**
- use a **variety of sentence types** to make your writing more interesting
- include a **concluding sentence**

ACTIVITY 1 | Identifying topic sentences and supporting sentences

Read the topics and sentences. Then write T for *topic sentence* or S for *supporting sentence*.

1. Kennedy Space Center

_____ **a.** You can take a tour of the rocket launch areas and participate in an astronaut training program.

_____ **b.** The Kennedy Space Center is an exciting place to visit.

2. Patience

_____ **a.** A teacher often shows patience to young students at the end of the school day.

_____ **b.** Patience is the ability to continue doing something even if you do not see any results immediately.

3. The Golden Gate Bridge

_____ **a.** The Golden Gate Bridge is famous worldwide.

_____ **b.** When it opened, it was the longest and tallest bridge of its kind in the world.

4. Making New Friends

_____ **a.** Many kids already have a group of friends from previous years.

_____ **b.** Making friends in a new school is hard.

5. Cell Phones and Driving

_____ **a.** When drivers talk or text on cell phones, they become distracted and do not pay enough attention to driving.

_____ **b.** Cell phones can be a danger to safe driving.

ACTIVITY 2 | Writing concluding sentences

Choose three topic sentences from Activity 1. Write a concluding sentence to go with each one.

1. _____

2. _____

3. _____

ACTIVITY 3 | Organizing sentences

Put the sentences in paragraph order (1 to 7). Then write an appropriate title.

Title: _____

a. _____ Instead, breakfast for them often consists of eggs with toast and coffee.

b. _____ People in Malaysia eat rice for breakfast, too, but their rice is cooked in coconut milk.

c. _____ Breakfast foods vary from country to country.

d. _____ However, people in most countries in Central and South America do not eat rice for breakfast.

e. _____ People eat this sweet, flavored rice with a red paste that is made of ground chili peppers and other ingredients.

f. _____ In Japan, for example, it is common to eat rice, soup, and fish for breakfast.

g. _____ From these varied breakfast items, it is clear that breakfast foods are different around the world.

A traditional
Japanese breakfast

ACTIVITY 4 | Choosing the correct verb

Choose the correct form of the verb in parentheses. Then answer the questions that follow.

WORDS TO KNOW Paragraph 8.1

entertainment: (n) amusement, fun
let: (v) to allow, permit
live: (adj) viewed by an audience as it happens

sunset: (n) the moment when the sun goes down
weak: (adj) not strong

PARAGRAPH 8.1

An Important Invention

The light bulb is one of the most important inventions of all time. In the past, people [1] (use / used) candles to see at night. This light was very **weak** and difficult to see with. However, now the light bulb [2] (**lets** / will let) us see things easily in the dark. This invention also [3] (helps / will help) us to do more work in one day. Before the light bulb, most work [4] (ends / ended) at **sunset**. Now people can continue to work outdoors or in their offices after the sun goes down. In addition, people can [5] (enjoy / enjoyed) **live entertainment** when it is dark. For example, sports fans [6] (watch / watched) games at night on lighted fields, and music lovers [7] (listen / listened) to concerts in lighted stadiums. Without the invention of the light bulb, our lives would be very different.

---

1. Underline the words that helped you choose the correct verb form.

2. What three reasons does the writer give to support the main idea?

a. _____

b. _____

c. _____

3. What information do the topic sentence and concluding sentence share?

_____

ACTIVITY 5 | Writing a paragraph

What do you think is an important invention in history? Write a short paragraph about it on a separate piece of paper. Use Paragraph 8.1 as a model.

ACTIVITY 6 | Using articles

Choose the correct articles to complete the paragraph.

> **WORDS TO KNOW** Paragraph 8.2
>
> **adventure:** (n) an exciting time or event
> **equipment:** (n) item(s) needed for a specific purpose
>
> **experience:** (n) an event or happening
> **unforgettable:** (adj) easy to remember

An Underwater Adventure

I will never forget my first **experience** with scuba diving. I was 19, and I was visiting Australia with my family. My father and I went scuba diving on [1](a / the / Ø) Great Barrier Reef. We went out to [2](a / the / Ø) reef with many other tourists on [3](a / an / the) special boat. When we got to [4](a / the / Ø) reef, the scuba diving instructor helped us put on our **equipment**. Then we dove into [5](a / the / Ø) clear blue water. Everything was so beautiful! There were [6](a / the / Ø) colorful fish and many different kinds of coral[1]. I swam everywhere. Suddenly, I saw [7](a / an / the) huge grey shark swimming toward me. I looked around for my father, but I was far away from him and [8](a / an / the) group of tourists. [9](A / An / The) shark got closer and closer. I was so scared that I could not move. Just when I thought that it might bite me, [10](a / an / the) shark turned and swam [11](a / the / Ø) other way. I quickly found my father. Scuba diving is always an **adventure**, but my first time was truly **unforgettable**.

[1]coral: a type of brightly colored stone made of tiny sea animals

A woman scuba diving on the Great Barrier Reef

ACTIVITY 7 | Combining sentences

Combine each pair of underlined simple sentences into a compound sentence on the lines below. Use the connecting words *and, but,* or *so* and a comma.

> **WORDS TO KNOW** Paragraph 8.3
>
> **jealous:** (adj) wanting something belonging to another person
> **passenger:** (n) a person who rides in a bus, boat, car, taxi, etc.
>
> **pedestrian:** (n) any person walking on a sidewalk, across the street, or down the road
> **powerful:** (adj) strong or effective, having great force

PARAGRAPH 8.3

My First Car

My first car made me a popular teenager. It was a Mustang. My Mustang was bright blue and very **powerful**. All my friends were **jealous** when they saw it. [1] They wanted to drive it. I told them they could not. I said that they could be **passengers** or **pedestrians**. [2] My friends did not want to walk. They were always passengers. However, the best thing about my car was the way it made me feel. [3] Every weekend, I drove to the movie theater. Every weekend, my friends rode with me. We felt like movie stars because everyone stared[1] at us in my beautiful blue car. I'll never forget how much fun I had with my friends in that cool car.

[1]stare: to look at someone or something steadily

A couple drives in the first Mustang ever sold.

1. _____

2. _____

3. _____

ACTIVITY 8 | Editing for compound sentences

Exchange the paragraph you wrote for Activity 5 with a partner. Check and edit your partner's compound sentences. If the paragraph does not have any compound sentences, suggest how to include one or two in the final draft.

ACTIVITY 9 | Identifying complex sentences

Underline all the complex sentences. Then answer the questions that follow.

WORDS TO KNOW Paragraph 8.4

collapse: (v) to fall down because of a lack of support

remove: (v) to move or take something away

set off: (phr v) to cause something accidentally

weight: (n) the measure of how heavy something is

PARAGRAPH 8.4

Earthquakes Caused by Humans

[1] Several types of human activity can **set off** earthquakes. [2] First, mining[1] can cause earthquakes. [3] When we **remove** dirt from the ground to build mines, the earth can become weak. [4] If it **collapses**, an earthquake can happen. [5] Next, humans can cause earthquakes by building dams[2]. [6] The **weight** of so much water in one place can set off an earthquake. [7] In addition, earthquakes can happen because fracking[3] is used to get oil or gas from the ground. [8] When the water that comes up with the oil or natural gas is put back into the ground, it can cause an earthquake. [9] If we continue to dig mines, build dams, and use fracking, we will have more and more earthquakes.

[1]mining: the business and process of taking minerals out of the earth
[2]dam: a barrier that keeps a river from flowing
[3]fracking: the process of adding water to underground rocks in order to get oil or gas

A hydro fracking tower used for gas drilling in Pennsylvania, USA

---

1. Which sentences have time clauses? _____

2. Which sentences have *if* clauses? _____

3. Which sentence has a reason clause? _____

ACTIVITY 10 | Editing for complex sentences

Exchange the paragraph you wrote for Activity 5 with a partner. Check and edit your partner's complex sentences. If the paragraph does not have any complex sentences, suggest how to include one or two in the final draft.

ACTIVITY 11 | Identifying adjective clauses

Underline all of the adjective clauses. Then circle the nouns that they describe.

> **WORDS TO KNOW** Paragraph 8.5
>
> **actually:** (adv) really; in truth or fact   **festival:** (n) a celebration on a special occasion
> **be in charge (of):** (phr) to have responsibility for

PARAGRAPH 8.5

How the Months of the Year Got Their Names

The names of all twelve months come from ancient culture and myths[1]. There are several months that are named after gods and goddesses. The first month, January, gets its name from the Roman god who **was in charge of** doors and beginnings—Janus. The name *March* comes from the Roman god of war, Mars. Some people believe that April is named after the Greek goddess of love, Aphrodite. May is named after Maia, a Greek earth goddess, and June is named after the Roman goddess who was connected to love and marriage—Juno. February gets its name from an old Roman **festival**. It is the only month that is named after a special occasion. Two months get their names from Roman emperors. July is named after Julius Caesar, and August is named for Emperor Augustus. The last four months of the year are named for where they were in the Roman calendar. *Septem, octo, novem,* and *decem* mean *seven, eight, nine,* and *ten* in Latin. September, October, November, and December were the seventh, eighth, ninth, and tenth months of the Roman calendar. The names of the months seem so common, but they **actually** have a long history.

[1]myth: a story from ancient societies about history, gods, or heroes

---

ACTIVITY 12 | Editing for adjective clauses

Exchange the paragraph you wrote for Activity 5 with a partner. Check and edit your partner's adjective clauses. If the paragraph does not have any adjective clauses, suggest how to include one or two in the final draft.

ACTIVITY 13 | Writing a final draft

Review all of the edits and suggestions that your partner(s) gave you for your paragraph from Activity 5. Write your final draft on a separate piece of paper.

BUILDING BETTER VOCABULARY

WORDS TO KNOW

actually (adv)	equipment (n) **AW**	live (adj)	set off (phr v)
adventure (n)	experience (n)	passenger (n)	sunset (n)
be in charge (of) (phr)	festival (n)	pedestrian (n)	unforgettable (adj)
collapse (v) **AW**	jealous (adj)	powerful (adj)	weak (adj)
entertainment (n)	let (v)	remove (v) **AW**	weight (n)

ACTIVITY 14 | Word associations

Circle the word or phrase that is more closely related to the bold word or phrase on the left.

1.	**actually**	hardly	really
2.	**be in charge (of)**	control	cause
3.	**jealous**	give	want
4.	**let**	allow	stop
5.	**passenger**	driver	rider
6.	**pedestrian**	walking	sitting
7.	**remove**	take away	put back
8.	**set off**	stop	start
9.	**sunset**	down	up
10.	**weak**	able	unable

ACTIVITY 15 | Collocations

Fill in the blank with the word that most naturally completes the phrase.

adventure	equipment	live	passengers	pedestrians

1. a _____ show

2. _____ on a plane

3. stop for _____

4. need special _____

5. an exciting _____

| experience | festival | powerful | sunset | weight |

6. lose _____

7. a film _____

8. an unforgettable _____

9. from sunrise to _____

10. a _____ engine

ACTIVITY 16 | Word forms

Complete each sentence with the correct word form. Use the correct form of the nouns and verbs.

NOUN	VERB	ADJECTIVE	SENTENCE PRACTICE
adventure		adventurous	**1.** My _____ cousin will eat anything. **2.** For small children, every day is a new _____ .
entertainment	entertain	entertaining	**3.** A big city offers a variety of _____ . **4.** The book is very _____ and will be made into a movie soon.
experience	experience	experienced	**5.** Virtual reality lets you _____ the world in a new way. **6.** Going away to college was a great _____ .
jealousy		jealous	**7.** _____ is a very strong emotion. **8.** My friends are all _____ of my new car.
power	power	powerful	**9.** Race horses are extremely _____ . **10.** Professional swimmers need a lot of physical _____ .

ACTIVITY 17 | Vocabulary in writing

Choose five words from Words to Know. Write a complete sentence with each word.

1. _____

2. _____

3. _____

4. _____

5. _____

BUILDING BETTER SENTENCES

ACTIVITY 18 | Editing

The paragraph has nine errors. Find and correct them.

2 comma errors	2 possessive adjective errors	1 verb form error
1 connecting word error	2 verb agreement errors	1 word order error

PARAGRAPH 8.6

The Island of the Colorblind

There are something unusual about Pingelap Atoll, a small island in the South Pacific. About 10 percent of their population is colorblind. This means they cannot see most or all colors. When a storm terrible hit the island in 1775 it kills most of the islanders. Because the population were so small the gene[1] for colorblindness passed to a lot of people over the next several hundred years. Theirs condition is known as achromatopsia. Some of the people on Pingelap who have achromatopsia are able to see colors like red and blue, so others only see black and white. People's understanding of color is certainly different on Pingelap Atoll.

[1]gene: the basic part of a living cell that contains characteristics of one's parents

ACTIVITY 19 | Writing sentences

Write an original sentence using the words listed.

1. (unforgettable/experience) _____

2. (extraordinary/achievement) _____

3. (typical/mistake) _____

4. (modern/machine) _____

5. (festival/celebrate) _____

ACTIVITY 20 | Combining sentences

Combine the ideas into one sentence. You may change the word forms, but do not change or omit any ideas. There may be more than one answer.

1. China has a festival.
   It happens every year in April.
   The festival is to celebrate a building project.
   The project changed the flow of the Min River.

   _____

   _____

2. There are underground tunnels.
   These tunnels are in parts of Argentina and Brazil.
   They were made by now-extinct animals.

   _____

   _____

3. Tasmania is a dangerous place to surf.
   There are great white sharks.
   There are waves up to 20 feet high.

   _____

   _____

WRITING

ACTIVITY 21 | Writing a paragraph

Some people think that e-books are better than paper books. Others disagree. What is your opinion? Write a paragraph that answers this question and gives your reasons. Follow these steps for writing. Put a check (√) next to each step as you complete it. Additionally, use a variety of sentence types and at least two vocabulary words or phrases presented in the unit. Underline the vocabulary.

1. _____ State your opinion in your topic sentence.

2. _____ Use sequence words to introduce each of your reasons.

3. _____ In your concluding sentence, restate your opinion or make a suggestion.

Editing

After you finish your writing, check your work for mistakes. Use the checklist below to help you.

- ☐ My topic sentence states my opinion and is indented.
- ☐ I wrote a sufficient number of supporting sentences related to the topic.
- ☐ I used sequence words to introduce each of my reasons.
- ☐ I wrote a concluding sentence that restates my opinion or makes a suggestion.
- ☐ I used simple, compound, and complex sentences.
- ☐ I gave my paragraph a title.

ACTIVITY 22 | Peer editing

Exchange papers from Activity 21 with a partner. Read your partner's paragraph. Then use Peer Editing Form 2 in the *Writer's Handbook* to help you comment on your partner's paragraph.

Additional Topics for Writing

Choose one or more of the topics to write about. Follow your teacher's directions.

TOPIC 1: Some people post photos of their children on social media. Other people do not think this is a good idea. What do you think? Why?

TOPIC 2: Do you think that crying is a sign of strength or a sign of weakness? Why?

TOPIC 3: Some schools require students to wear uniforms. Do you think this is a good idea? Why or why not?

TOPIC 4: Locavores are people who believe it is good to only eat food that is grown very close to where they live. They believe this helps the environment and local farmers. How do you feel about this idea?

TOPIC 5: Think of a situation that people are currently debating in your school, community, or city. Why do people disagree about this situation? What is your opinion?

TEST PREP

You should spend about 25 minutes on this task. Write a paragraph with six to ten sentences.

Nothing worth doing is easy. Do you agree or disagree with this statement?

Remember to indent your paragraph, include a topic sentence, develop the main idea with supporting sentences, use a variety of sentence types, and include a concluding sentence.

> **TIP**
> Leave time to review your writing. Check that you answered the question, provided enough supporting sentences, organized your ideas clearly, and included the four main parts of a paragraph. Review your grammar, spelling, and punctuation.

WRITER'S HANDBOOK

LANGUAGE TERMS

Adjective   An adjective describes a noun.

Lexi is a very **smart** girl.

Adverb   An adverb describes a verb, an adjective, or another adverb.

The secretary types **quickly**. She types **very quickly**.

Article   Articles are used with nouns. The definite article is *the*. The indefinite articles are *a* and *an*.

The teacher gave **an** assignment to **the** students.

Clause   A clause is a group of words that has a subject-verb combination. Sentences can have one or more clauses.

<u>Roger attends</u> the College of New Jersey.
clause

<u>Chris needs</u> to study <u>because he wants</u> to pass the class.
clause 1   clause 2

Complex Sentence   A complex sentence consists of an independent clause and a dependent clause. Dependent clauses include time clauses, *if* clauses, and reasons clauses.

<u>We will go to lunch</u> <u>as soon as class is over</u>.
ind clause   dep clause

<u>If you miss the test,</u> <u>you cannot take it again</u>.
dep clause   ind clause

<u>Chris studies hard</u> <u>because he wants to do well</u>.
ind clause   dep clause

Compound Sentence   A compound sentence consists of two simple sentences that are joined by a comma and a connector such as *and*, *but*, or *so*.

<u>I love to study English</u>**,** **but** <u>my sister prefers math</u>.
simple sentence 1   simple sentence 2

Dependent Clause   A dependent clause is a group of words with a subject-verb combination that cannot be a sentence by itself. It starts with a connector such as *before*, *after*, *if*, or *because*.

I am taking a lot of science classes **because I want to go to medical school**.

Independent Clause	An independent clause is a group of words with a subject-verb combination that can be a sentence by itself. **I am taking a lot of science classes** because I want to go to medical school.
Noun	A noun is a person, place, thing, or idea. The **students** are reading **poems** about **friendship** and **love**.
Object	An object is a word that comes after a transitive verb or a preposition. It is often a noun, noun phrase, pronoun, or gerund. Jim bought **a new car**. I left my jacket in **the house**.
Phrase	A phrase is a small group of words that create a larger unit, such as a noun phrase or prepositional phrase. Kimchi is **a traditional Korean dish**. Jane forgot her phone **on the bus**.
Preposition	A preposition is a word that shows location, time, or direction. Prepositions are often one word (*at, on, in*), but they can also consist of two words (*in between*) or three words (*on top of*). The university is **in** the center of the city.

Pronoun	A pronoun can replace a noun in a sentence. Using a combination of nouns and pronouns adds variety to your writing.
	
	   n subj pronoun
	Whales are mammals. **They** breathe air.
	        n obj pronoun
	Some **whales** are endangered. We need to protect **them**.

Punctuation	Punctuation refers to the marks used in writing to separate sentences and parts of sentences and to clarify meaning. The colors of the American flag are red, white, and blue, and the colors of the Mexican flag are red, white, and green.
Subject	The subject of a sentence tells who or what a sentence is about. It is often a noun, noun phrase, pronoun, or gerund. **My teacher** gave us a homework assignment. **It** was difficult.

VERB FORMS

VERB FORM AND USE	AFFIRMATIVE	NEGATIVE
Simple Present • regular activities or habits • facts or things that are generally true • a process (how to make or do something)	I/you/we/they **work** he/she/it **works** *Be:* I **am** you/we/they **are** he/she/it **is**	I/you/we/they **do not work** he/she/it **does not work** *Be:* I **am not** you/we/they **are not** he/she/it **is not**
Simple Past • recent or historical events • a narrative, or story, that is real or imagined • events in a person's life • result of an experiment	I/you/we/they **worked** he/she/it **worked** *Be:* I **was** You/we/they **were** He/she/it **was**	I/you/we/they **did not work** he/she/it **did not work** *Be:* I **was not** You/we/they **were not** He/she/it **was not**
Present Progressive • actions that are currently in progress • future actions if a future time expression is used or understood	I **am working** you/we/they **are working** he/she/it **is working**	I **am not working** you/we/they **are not working** he/she/it **is not working**
Future with *be going to* • future plans that are already made • predictions that are based on a present action	I **am going to go** you/we/they **are going to go** he/she/it **is going to go**	I **am not going to go** you/we/they **are not going to go** he/she/it **is not going to go**
Future with *will* • future plans/decisions made in the moment • strong predictions • promises and offers to help	I/you/we/they **will go** he/she/it **will go**	I/you/we/they **will not go** he/she/it **will not go**
Present Perfect • actions that began in the past and continue until the present • actions that happened at an indefinite time in the past • when a time period is not complete	I/you/we/they **have worked** he/she/it **has worked**	I/you/we/they **have not worked** he/she/it **has not worked**

CAPITALIZATION AND PUNCTUATION

Capitalization

Capitalize:

- the first word in a sentence

    We go to the movies every week.
    Deserts are beautiful places to visit.

- the pronoun *I*

    Larry and **I** are brothers

- people's formal and professional titles

    Mr. and **M**rs. Jenkins are on vacation.
    Lisa saw **D**r. Johansen at the bank yesterday.

- proper names (specific people, places, and things)

    Kate met her brother **A**lex at the park.
    The **C**oliseum in **R**ome is a beautiful old monument.
    Nick is taking **H**istory 101 this semester.

- names of streets.

    Ruth lives on **W**ilson **A**venue.

- geographical locations (cities, states, countries, continents, lakes, and rivers)

    I am going to travel to **L**ondon, **E**ngland, next week.
    The **A**rno **R**iver passes through **T**uscany, **I**taly.

- the names of languages and nationalities

    My grandmother speaks Polish.
    Melissa is Venezuelan, but her husband is Cuban.

- most words in titles of paragraphs, essays, and books

    The Life of Billy Barnes
    Into the Wild

Commas

Use a comma:

- before the connectors *and*, *but*, *so*, and *or* in a compound sentence

   Rick bought Julia a croissant, but she wanted a muffin.

- between three or more items in a list

   Jen brought a towel, an umbrella, some sunscreen, and a book to the beach.

- after a dependent clause at the beginning of a complex sentence. Dependent clauses include time clauses, *if* clauses, and reason clauses

   Because it was raining outside, Alex used his umbrella.

- between the day and the date and between the date and the year

   The last day of class will be Friday, May 19th.
   I was born on June 27, 1992.

- between and after (if in the middle of a sentence) city, state, and country names that appear together

   The concert was in Busan, Korea.
   I lived in Phuket, Thailand, for ten years.

- after time words and phrases, prepositional phrases of time, and sequence words (except *then*) at the start of a sentence

   Every afternoon after school, I go to the library.
   Finally, they decided to ask the police for help.

SPELLING

-*S* Form Verbs and Plural Nouns

- Add *s* to most verbs to make the -*s* form, and to most nouns to make them plural.

   student—students   teacher—teachers   apple—apples

- If a verb or noun ends in *ss*, *sh*, *ch*, *z*, or *x*, add *es*.

   class—classes   brush—brushes   watch—watches   buzz—buzzes   box—boxes

- If a verb or noun ends in a consonant + *y*, change the *y* to *i* and add *es*.

   party—parties   lady—ladies   library—libraries

- If a verb or noun ends in a vowel + *y*, do not change the *y*. Just add *s*.

   boy—boys   day—days   toy—toys

Regular Simple Past Verbs

- Add *ed* to the base form of most verbs.

    start—started   finish—finished   wash—washed

- Add only *d* when the base form ends in *e*.

    live—lived   care—cared   die—died

- If a verb ends in a consonant + *y*, change the *y* to *i* and add *ed*.

    dry—dried   carry—carried   study—studied

- If a verb ends in a vowel + *y*, do not change the *y*. Just add *ed*.

    play—played   stay—stayed   destroy—destroyed

- If a verb has one syllable and ends in consonant + vowel + consonant (CVC), double the final consonant and add *ed*.

    stop—stopped   rob—robbed

- If a verb ends in a *w* or *x*, do not double the final consonant. Just add *ed*.

    sew—sewed   mix—mixed

- If a verb that ends in CVC has two syllables and the second syllable is stressed, double the final consonant and add *ed*.

    ad**mit**—admitted   oc**cur**—occurred   per**mit**—permitted

- If a verb that ends in CVC has two syllables and the first syllable is stressed, do not double the final consonant. Just add *ed*.

    happen—happened   **lis**ten—listened   **o**pen—opened

IRREGULAR SIMPLE PAST VERBS

Here are some common irregular verbs in English.

BASE FORM	PAST	BASE FORM	PAST	BASE FORM	PAST
be	was/were	find	found	see	saw
become	became	flee	fled	sell	sold
begin	began	forget	forgot	send	sent
bite	bit	get	got	set	set
bleed	bled	give	gave	sing	sang
blow	blew	grow	grew	sink	sank
break	broke	have	had	sit	sat
bring	brought	hear	heard	sleep	slept
build	built	hide	hid	speak	spoke
buy	bought	hit	hit	spend	spent
catch	caught	hold	held	stand	stood
choose	chose	hurt	hurt	steal	stole
come	came	keep	kept	swim	swam
cost	cost	know	knew	take	took
cut	cut	leave	left	teach	taught
do	did	let	let	tell	told
draw	drew	lose	lost	think	thought
drink	drank	make	made	throw	threw
drive	drove	pay	paid	understand	understood
eat	ate	put	put	wear	wore
fall	fell	read	read	win	won
feel	felt	run	ran	write	wrote
fight	fought	say	said		

ARTICLES

A and *An*

Use *a* or *an* before a singular count noun when its meaning is general. Use *a* before a word that starts with a consonant sound. Use *an* before a word that starts with a vowel sound.

Words that begin with the letters *h* and *u* can take *a* or *an* depending on their opening sound.

- When the *h* is pronounced, use *a*.

    a horse / **a** hat / **a** hot day / **a** huge dog

- When the *h* is silent, use *an*.

    an hour / **an** honor / **an** honorable man / **an** herbal tea

- When the *u* sounds like *you*, use *a* (because the first sound in the word is a vowel sound).

    a university / **a** uniform / **a** useful invention / **a** unique idea

- When the *u* sounds like *uh*, use *an*.

    an umpire / **an** umbrella / **an** ugly shirt **/ an** uncomfortable chair

The

Use *the*:

- before a singular count noun, plural count noun, or non-count noun when its meaning is specific

    I need to ask my parents to borrow **the** <u>car</u> today.

- the second (and third, fourth, etc.) time you write about something

    I bought a new coat yesterday. **The** <u>coat</u> is blue and gray.

- when the noun you are referring to is unique—there is only one

    The <u>Sun</u> and **the** <u>Earth</u> are both in **the** <u>Milky Way Galaxy</u>.
    The <u>Eiffel Tower</u> is a beautiful monument.

- with specific time periods

    You must be very quiet for **the** <u>next hour</u>.
    The <u>1920s</u> was a time of great change in the United States.

- when other words in your sentence make the noun specific

  The <u>cat in the picture</u> is very pretty.

- with geographic locations that end in the plural *s* (such as a group of islands), or that include the words *united*, *union*, *kingdom*, or *republic*

  We are going to **the** <u>Bahamas</u> for our vacation.
  Who is the president of **the** <u>United States</u>?

- with most buildings, bodies of water (except lakes), mountain chains, and deserts

  The <u>White House</u> is in Washington, DC.
  The <u>Amazon</u> is a very long river in South America.

Do not use *the*:

- with the names of cities, states, countries, continents, and lakes (except as mentioned above)

  Sylvie is from <u>Venezuela</u>. She lives near <u>Lake Maracaibo</u>.
  <u>Lake Baikal</u> is a large freshwater lake in Russia.

- before names or when you talk about something in general

  <u>Mikhail Bulgakov</u> is a famous Russian writer.
  <u>Jason</u> is going to make a table with <u>wood</u>.

NOUNS AND PRONOUNS

Common Non-count Nouns

Count nouns can be counted. They have a singular form (*phone*, *person*) and a plural form (*phones*, *people*). Non-count nouns are not countable. They have only one form (money, information).

Here are some common non-count nouns.

COMMON NON-COUNT NOUNS	
Food items	butter, sugar, salt, pepper, soup, rice, fish, meat, flour, bread
Liquids	milk, coffee, water, juice, cream
Academic subjects	English, math, science, music, biology
Abstract ideas	love, honesty, poverty, crime, advice, luck, pain, hate, beauty, humor
Others	homework, information, money, furniture, traffic

Possessive Pronouns

A possessive pronoun takes the place of a possessive adjective + noun combination. Possessive adjectives + nouns and possessive pronouns can be in the subject or object position.

POSSESSIVE ADJECTIVE + NOUN	POSSESSIVE PRONOUN
The pencil on the table is **my pencil**.	The pencil on the table is **mine**.
Because I left my book at home, I need to share **your book** with you.	Because I left my book at home, I need to share **yours** with you.
My ring is silver, but **his ring** is gold.	My ring is silver, but **his** is gold.
Carol has my cell phone, and I have **her cell phone**.	Carol has my cell phone, and I have **hers**.
Your room is on the first floor, and **our room** is on the fifth floor.	Your room is on the first floor, and **ours** is on the fifth floor.
Our class got to have a special party, but **your class** did not.	Our class got to have a special party, but **yours** did not.
Jenny likes her class, and Karl and Jim like **their class**, too.	Jenny likes her class, and Karl and Jim like **theirs**, too.

Quantifiers

Quantifiers give more information about the number, or quantity, of a noun. They usually go in front of a noun.

QUANTIFIER	EXAMPLE
With Count Nouns	
one, two, three (all numbers)	**Several** students went to the school office. **Many** people wanted to leave the city. Ellie put **a few** coins in the parking meter.
a few	
few	
many	
another	
several	
a pair of	
a couple of	
With Non-count Nouns	
a little	There is only **a little** milk left in the refrigerator. We get too **much** homework every night.
little	
much	
With Count or Non-count Nouns	
some	Mrs. Jones has **a lot of** friends. They got into **a lot of** trouble. I do not have **any** plans for this weekend. Adam does not have **any** money.
any	
a lot of	

ORDER OF ADJECTIVES

In general, there are seven categories of adjectives. When you use more than one adjective to describe a noun, use the following order.

1. size   small, large, huge
2. opinion   beautiful, nice, ugly
3. shape   round, square, oval
4. condition   broken, damaged, burned
5. age   old, young, new
6. color   red, white, green
7. origin   French, American, Korean

✓ He has an enormous brown dog.

✗ He has a <u>brown enormous</u> dog.

You can also use more than one adjective from the same category. Put a comma in between these adjectives, or use *and*. Use *and* when the adjectives follow a linking verb.

She is a shy, quiet girl.
She is a shy and quiet girl.
She is shy and quiet.

PREPOSITIONS

At, On, and *In*

Prepositions indicate time, location, and direction. Prepositions are always the first word in a prepositional phrase, which is a preposition + noun.

Three common prepositions in English are *at*, *on*, and *in*.

Using *At*

Location: Use *at* for specific locations.

Angela works **at** the First National Bank.
I always do my homework **at** my desk.
Joel met Jillian **at** the corner of Polk Street and Florida Avenue.

Time: Use *at* for specific times.

> My grammar class meets **at** 9:00 a.m. every day.
> The lunch meeting begins **at** noon.
> Cate does not like to walk alone **at** night.

Direction: Use *at* for motion toward a goal.

> My brother threw a ball **at** me.
> The robber pointed his gun **at** the policewoman.

Using *On*

Location: Use *on* when there is contact between two objects.

> The picture is **on** the wall.
> He put his books **on** the kitchen table.
> Erin lives **on** Bayshore Boulevard.

Time: Use *on* with specific days or dates.

> Our soccer game is **on** Saturday.
> Your dentist appointment is **on** October 14.
> I was born **on** June 22, 1988.

Using *In*

Location: Use *in* when something is inside another thing.

> The books are **in** the big box.
> I left my jacket **in** your car.
> Barbara lives **in** Istanbul.

Time: Use *in* for a specific period of time, a specific year, or a future time.

> I am going to graduate from college **in** three years.
> My best friend got married **in** 2006.
> Mr. Johnson always drinks four cups of coffee **in** the morning.
> We will meet you **in** ten minutes.

Other Prepositions

Here are more common prepositions and prepositional phrases of location. In the chart on the next page, the preposition or prepositional phrase shows the location of the ball in relation to the box.

PREPOSITION		EXAMPLE
under		Pedro keeps his shoes **under** his bed.
above/over		Sheila held the umbrella **over** her head.
between		The milk is **between** the eggs and the butter.
in front of		Mark was standing in **front of** the restaurant.
in back of/behind		My shirt fell **behind** my dresser.
across…from		There is a supermarket **across** the street **from** my house.
next to/beside		The mailman left the package **next to** the door.

CONNECTORS

Connectors in Compound Sentences

Connectors in compound sentences are called coordinating conjunctions. They are used to connect two independent clauses. A comma usually appears before a connector that separates two independent clauses in a compound sentence.

COORDINATING CONJUNCTION	PURPOSE	EXAMPLE
and	to add information	Miki works full time, **and** she is a student.
but	to show contrast	The exam was hard, **but** everyone passed.
so	to show a result	It was raining, **so** we decided to stay home last night.
or	to give a choice	We can cook, **or** we can order pizza.
yet*	to show contrast/concession	There was a hurricane warning, **yet** many people went to the beach.
nor**	to add negative information	Roberto does not like opera, **nor** does he enjoy hip-hop.
for†	to show reason	He ate a sandwich, **for** he was hungry.

*Yet is similar to but; however, it usually shows a stronger or unexpected contrast.
**Question word order is used in the clause that follows nor.
†The conjunction for is not commonly used except in literary writing.

Many writers remember these connectors in compound sentences (or coordinating conjunctions) with the acronym *FANBOYS*: F = *for*, A = *and*, N = *nor*, B = *but*, O = *or*, Y = *yet*, and S = *so*.

Connectors in Complex Sentences

Connectors in complex sentences are called subordinating conjunctions. They are used to connect a dependent clause and an independent clause. Use a comma after a dependent clause when it is at the beginning of a sentence.

SUBORDINATING CONJUNCTION	PURPOSE	EXAMPLE
because since as	to show reason/cause	He ate a sandwich **because/since/as** he was hungry.
although even though though while	to show contrast	**Although/Even though/Though** the exam was difficult, everyone passed. Deborah is a dentist **while** John is a doctor.
after as as soon as before until while when	to show a time relationship	**After** we ate dinner, we went to a movie. **As** I was leaving the office, it started to rain. **As soon as** class ended, Mia ran out the door. We ate dinner **before** we went to a movie. I will not call you **until** I finish studying. **While** the pasta is cooking, I will cut the vegetables. **When** Jennifer gets home, she is going to eat dinner.
if even if	to show condition	**If** it rains tomorrow, we will stay home. We are going to go to the park **even if** it rains tomorrow.

EDITING YOUR WRITING

One way to improve your writing is to ask someone for feedback. Another way is to check your own work. You should read your work to make sure that it:

- responds to the assignment
- has a title
- has a topic sentence
- has sufficient supporting sentences
- has a concluding sentence
- is free from errors

This section will help you become more familiar with how to identify and correct errors in your writing.

Step 1

Below is a student's first draft paragraph for a writing assignment. The prompt for this assignment was "Write about a very happy or a very sad event in your life." As you read the paragraph, use the points above to look for areas that need improvement. For example, does the paragraph have a topic sentence? Do the supporting sentences actually support the topic sentence? Does every sentence have a subject and a verb? Does the writer always use the correct verb form and the correct punctuation?

My Saddest Day

The day I came for the U.S. is my saddest. That night my family gave me a big party. We staied up all night. In the morning, all the people were go to the airport. We cryed and said good-bye. they kissed and huged me. i think that i will not see them ever again. i was sad in united states for six months. now i feel better. that was my saddest day.

Step 2

Read the teacher comments on the first draft of "My Saddest Day." Are these the same things that you noticed?

My Saddest Day

Remember to indent   was
The day I came for the U.S. is my saddest. That night my family gave me a big party.

        spelling   verb form   spelling
We staied up all night. In the morning, all the people were go to the airport. We cryed

and said good-bye. they kissed and huged me. i think that i will not see them ever

            Always put "the" in front of "United States"
again. i was sad in united states for six months. now i feel better. that was my saddest day.

You have some good ideas in this paragraph. I really like your topic sentence and concluding sentence. However, you write about three different time frames. You write about the night you left your country, the day you arrived in the United States, and six months after you arrived. Choose one of these times and write about that. I'd really like to learn about your party.

Verbs: You must review the spelling rules for the simple past tense. You had a very hard time with this. Also, be careful with irregular forms. The incorrect forms distract from your ideas. I corrected your first mistake. Fix the others I've circled.

I underlined some capitalization errors. Please fix these, too.

Step 3

Now read the second draft of this paragraph. How is it the same as the first draft? How is it different? Did the writer fix all the errors?

My Saddest Day

The night before I came for the U.S. was my saddest day. That night my family gave me a big party. All my family and friends were come to it. We sang, danced, and ate many food. We stayed up all night. We talked about my new life. When everyone left, we cried and said good-bye. They kissed and hugged me. I think I will not see them ever again. Finally, I went to bed at 4:00 in the morning. However, I could not sleep because I was so sad. I was sad in the United States for six months. Now I feel better, but that was my saddest day.

USEFUL WORDS AND PHRASES

Try these useful words and phrases as you write your sentences and paragraphs. They can make your writing sound more academic, natural, and fluent.

STATING AN OPINION	
I believe/think/feel (that)… In my opinion/view,…	**I believe that** New York City should ban large sugary drinks. **In my opinion,** art classes are important.
…should (not) be allowed (…) …must/should/ought to…	Bringing your own snacks to a movie theater **should be allowed**. Researchers **must** stop unethical animal testing.
I agree/disagree (that)… I agree that… However,…	**I agree that** daylight saving time is not necessary anymore. **I agree that** eating healthily is important. **However,** the government should not make food choices for us.
…is the most/least… …is the best/worst… …is a/an…book/movie/article.	Thailand **is the most** interesting country in the world. Thailand **is the best** place to go on vacation. *Harry Potter and the Goblet of Fire* by J.K. Rowling **is an** entertaining **book**.
There are many benefits/advantages to…	**There are many benefits to** swimming every day.
There are many drawbacks/disadvantages to…	**There are many drawbacks to** eating most of your meals at a restaurant.

GIVING AND ADDING EXAMPLES AND SUPPORT

For example/instance,…	My instructor gives us so much homework. **For example**, yesterday he gave us five pages of grammar work.
According to…,…	**According to** a recent poll, 85 percent of high school students felt they had too much homework.
One example (of…) is…	There are several different types of runners. **One example is** a marathon runner.
Another example (of…) is… …is another example (of…)	**Another example of** a type of runner **is** a sprinter. A sprinter **is another example**.
…, such as…	There are many places to visit in New York City, **such as** the Statue of Liberty, the Empire State Building, and Central Park.

LISTING

First/Second/Third,… Next,… Last/Lastly/Finally,…	**Lastly,** you should visit my country because of its amazing mountains.
One reason to…is… One type of…is…	**One reason to** visit my country **is** the wonderful weather. **One type of** runner **is** a long-distance runner.
Another reason to…is… Another type of…is… …is another reason to… …is another type of…	**Another reason to** visit my country **is** the delicious food. The delicious food **is another reason to** visit my country.

DESCRIBING A PROCESS

First/Second/Next/Finally,… Then…	**First,** you cut the fish and vegetables into small pieces. **Next,** you add the lime juice. **Then** you add in the seasonings. **Finally,** mix everything together well.
The first/second/next/last thing you (need to) do is…	**The first thing you need to do is** wash your hands.
Before/After you…, you (need to)…	**Before you** cut up the vegetables, **you need to** wash them. **After you** cut up the vegetables, **you** add them to the salad.
After that, you (need to)…	**After that, you need to** mix the ingredients.
The first/next/final step is…	**The last step is** adding your favorite salad dressing.

TOPIC SENTENCES FOR PARAGRAPHS WITH LISTING ORDER

There are many/several/some…	**There are many** good places to visit in my country. **There are several** different types of runners.
…must/should/need(s) to follow a few/a couple of/three (simple/specific) steps…	A tourist **must follow four steps** to get a visa to visit my country. To take a good picture with your phone, you **need to follow a few simple steps**.
…for many/several/three reasons.	Art is an important subject to study **for several reasons**.

CONCLUDING SENTENCES

In conclusion,…	**In conclusion,** I believe that my parents are the best in the world.
For these reasons, I think/believe (that)…	**For these reasons, I think that** schools need to offer art classes every semester.
It is clear that…	**It is clear that** Guatemala is the best tourist destination in South America.
If you follow these steps,…	**If you follow these steps,** you will not need to call an expert.

SHOWING CAUSE AND EFFECT

Because…, … …because… Because of…,… …because of…	**Because** I broke my leg, I could not move. I could not move **because** I broke my leg. **Because of** my broken leg, I could not move. I could not move **because of** my broken leg.
…, so…	My sister did not know what to do, **so** she asked my mother for advice.

TELLING A STORY

I will never forget the day/month/year/time…	**I will never forget the day** I left my country.
I can still/will always remember the day/month/year/time…	**I can still remember the day** I started my first job.
…was the best/worst day/month/year of my life.	My sixteenth birthday **was the best day of my life**.

DESCRIBING

…tastes/looks/smells/feels like…	My ID card **looks like** a credit card.
…is known/famous for its…	France **is famous for its** cheese.

KEEPING A VOCABULARY JOURNAL

Vocabulary is very important to learning English. The best way for you to really improve your vocabulary is to do more than study from your teacher or this book. You should also keep a vocabulary journal.

A vocabulary journal is a notebook in which you write down all the new words and phrases that you do not know but you think are important. When you find a new word, write it in your notebook. However, writing words in the notebook is not enough. You also need to review the words many times.

The most important thing about learning vocabulary is the number of times you think about the word, listen to it, read it, speak it, or write it. You can practice any way you want.

There are many ways to organize a vocabulary journal, and you should choose a way that you like. It is important to remember this is your journal, and it should be useful for you. Here is one way to keep a vocabulary journal. You write four pieces of information about each new word, but you can write as little or as much as you want.

1. Write the English word first.
2. Write a translation in your first language.
3. Write a simple definition or synonym in English.
4. Write a phrase or sentence with the word. Use a blank (___) instead of writing the word.

With these four kinds of information, you can practice the new vocabulary four ways.

Leave a lot of white space between the words and the information you write. Each page of your notebook should have only five to eight words. As you learn new information about the word, you can write that information in the white space.

Here are two examples:

From a Spanish speaker's vocabulary journal:

dozen   12 things

docena   a _____ eggs

From an Arabic speaker's vocabulary journal:

hot   not cold

حار   The sun is very _____.

TEST TAKING TIPS

Here are some useful tips for taking timed writing tests.

Before Writing

- Before you begin writing, make sure that you understand the assignment. Underline key words in the writing prompt. Look back at the key words as you write to be sure you are answering the question correctly and staying on topic.

- Take five minutes to plan before you start writing. First, list out all the ideas you have about the topic. Then think about which ideas have the best supporting examples or ideas. Use this information to choose your main idea(s). Circle the supporting information you want to include. Cross out other information.

- Write on the assigned topic. Do not write more than is requested. If the assignment asks for a 150-word response, be sure that your writing response comes close to that. Students do not get extra points for writing more than what is required.

While Writing

- Be sure that you have a strong topic sentence. Remember that your topic sentence guides your paragraph. If the topic sentence is not clear, the reader will have difficulty following your supporting ideas.

- It is important for your writing to look like a paragraph. Be sure to indent the first sentence. Write the rest of the sentences from margin to margin. Leave an appropriate amount of space after your periods. These small details make your paragraph easier to read and understand.

- Organize your ideas before you write. Review the list you have created. Place a number next to each idea, from most important to least important. In this way, if you do not have enough time to complete your writing, you will be sure that the most relevant information will be included in your paragraph.

- Once you pick a side (agree or disagree), include only the ideas that support that side. Sometimes you may have ideas for both sides. If this happens, choose the side that is easier for you to write about. If you do not have an opinion, choose the side you can write about best, even if you do not believe in it. You receive points for your writing skill, not your true personal beliefs.

Word Choice

- Avoid using words such as *always*, *never*, *all*, and *none*. You cannot give enough proof for these words. Instead, use words such as *probably*, *often*, *most*, *many*, *almost never*, and *almost none*.

- Avoid using general or vague vocabulary. Words such as *nice*, *good*, and *very* can often be changed to more specific terms, such as *friendly*, *fabulous*, and *incredibly*. Be more specific in your word choice.

- Avoid slang and informal language in academic writing.

Development

- Avoid information that is too general. When possible, give specific examples. Good writers want to show that they have thought about the subject and provide interesting and specific information in their writing.

After Writing/Proofreading

- Leave time to review your writing. Proofread your paragraph and check for subject-verb agreement, correct use of commas and end punctuation, and for clear ideas that all relate to the topic sentence.

- Check for informal language like contractions or slang. These do not belong in academic writing.

PEER EDITING FORMS

Peer Editing Form 1

Reader: _____ Date: _____

1. Do the sentences answer the questions?   ☐ Yes   ☐ No

   If no, explain: _____

   _____

2. Do all the sentences

   a. have a subject and a verb?   ☐ Yes   ☐ No
   b. begin with a capital letter?   ☐ Yes   ☐ No
   c. end with a period?   ☐ Yes   ☐ No

   If *no*, explain: _____

   _____

   _____

3. Check all that apply: The writer correctly used

   ☐ the verb *be*

   ☐ *there is/there are*

   ☐ prepositional phrases of place

   ☐ capitalization with proper nouns

4. Is there any place where the information is unclear?   ☐ Yes   ☐ No

   If yes, where? _____

   _____

5. Is there any place where you want more information?   ☐ Yes   ☐ No

   If yes, where? _____

   _____

Peer Editing Form 2

Reader: _____ Date: _____

1. Does the paragraph have a title? □ Yes □ No

2. Does the paragraph have an indented first line? □ Yes □ No

3. Does the paragraph have a topic sentence? □ Yes □ No

    If yes, write it here: _____

    _____

4. Does the paragraph have a concluding sentence? □ Yes □ No

    If yes, write it here. Underline information connected to the topic sentence.

    _____

    _____

5. Is there any place you want more information? □ Yes □ No

    If yes, where? _____

6. Does the paragraph use at least two vocabulary words/phrases from the unit? □ Yes □ No

    List them here: _____

7. Does the paragraph have any mistakes with

    a. grammar? □ Yes □ No

    b. capitalization? □ Yes □ No

    c. punctuation? □ Yes □ No

    If yes, briefly explain here: _____

    _____

8. What do you like best about this paragraph? _____

    _____

VOCABULARY INDEX

Word	Page	CEFR† Level	Word	Page	CEFR† Level	Word	Page	CEFR† Level
pay attention	134	B1	routine	63	B1	taste	36	B1
pedestrian	170	B1	row	132	B1	tax	116	B1
perform	112	B1	scientist	8	B1	temporary*	63	B1
plan	36	A2	service	110	B1	the wild	134	A2
popular	18	A2	set off	171	B1	totally	116	B1
powerful	170	B1	sight	107	B1	tourist	18	A2
practice	14	A2	similar*	116	B1	traffic	34	A2
prize	84	A2	simple	12	A2	trend*	151	B1
produce	151	B1	skill	139	B1	typical	72	B1
project*	87	A2	solve	86	B1	unfair	155	B1
provide	153	B1	space	66	A2	unforgettable	169	B1
recycle	114	B1	special	112	B1	variety	18	A2
reduce	153	B1	spend	107	A2	weak	168	B1
relax*	30	B1	stressful*	63	B1	weight	171	B2
reliable*	18	B1	suffering	84	B2	well-known	66	A2
remove*	171	B1	suggestion	131	B1	whole	65	A2
research*	8	B1	sunset	168	B1	yell	92	B2

Every unit in *Great Writing* highlights key academic vocabulary, indicated by AW . These words have been selected using the Academic Word List (Coxhead, 2000) and the New Academic Word List (Browne, C., Culligan, B. & Phillips, J., 2013).

*These words are on the AWL or NAWL.

†Vocabulary was also chosen based on levels of The Common European Framework of Reference for Languages (CEFR). CEFR is an international standard for describing language proficiency. *Great Writing 1* is most appropriate for students at CEFR levels A2–B1.

The target vocabulary is at the CEFR levels as shown.

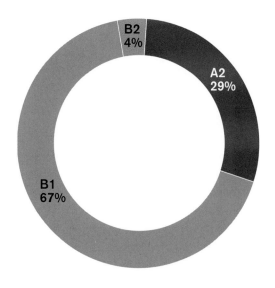

INDEX

O

Object adjective clauses, 133–134
Object of sentences, 4
Object pronouns, 44, 46
Opinion verbs, 154
Organizing ideas, 150

P

Paragraphs
  basics, 30–37, 166–167
  concluding sentence, 30, 48–49
  defined, 30
  organizing, 167
  response, 152–154, 162–163
  sequence words and phrases,
    150–151
  supporting sentences, 37
  topic sentences, 34
  writing process, 80–81
Past time words and phrases, 88–89
Peer editing, 25–27, 57, 80, 102,
  127, 146, 163, 177
Plagiarism, 153
Plural nouns, 73
Possessive adjectives, 47
Prepositional phrases
  be verbs with, 7
  there is/there are with, 12
  of time and place, 10–11
Pronouns
  of object, 44, 46
  of subject, 44–45
Proper nouns, capitalization of, 18
Punctuation, commas, 70–71, 96,
  121, 170

R

Reason clauses, 117–120
Response paragraphs, 152–154,
  162–163

S

Sentences
  be verbs in, 7
  capitalization of, 17
  complex, 95–97, 113–115, 119,
    171–172
  compound, 69–71, 119, 170
  concluding, 166–167
  fragments, 6
  future forms, 106–115
  if clauses, 116–117

noun and noun phrases, 7
  object of, 4
  prepositional phrases, 7, 10–11
  reason clauses, 117–120
  sequence words and phrases,
    150–151
  simple, 4, 69–70, 170
  simple past affirmative, 85–89
  simple past negative, 89–93
  simple present form, 60–63
  subject of, 4
  subordinating conjunctions, 95
  supporting, 152, 166
  topic sentences, 150, 152, 166
  using *It* as a subject, 6
  variety of, 130, 166
  verbs in, 4
Sequence words and phrases, 43,
  150–151
Simple past affirmative, 85–89
Simple past form, 84–93
Simple past negative form, 89–93
Simple present affirmative form,
  61–67
Simple present form, 60–63
Simple present negative form,
  67–68
Simple sentences, 4, 60–63, 69–70,
  85–93, 170
Singular nouns, 73
Subject
  in compound sentences, 69
  It as, 6
  plural, 66
  of sentence, 4
  simple past affirmative, 85–89
  simple present affirmative, 61–63
  simple present negative, 67–68
  in simple sentences, 69
  there are vs. *they are*, 66–67
Subject adjective clauses, 132–133
Subject pronouns, 44–45
Subject-verb combinations, 69
Subordinating conjunctions, 95
Supporting sentences, 37, 152, 166

T

Test Prep, 27, 57, 81, 103, 127, 147,
  163, 177
Time clauses, 95

Time words or phrases, 10–11,
  88–89, 112–115
Timed writing, 27, 57, 81, 103, 127,
  147, 163, 177
Titles, of paragraph, 32
Topic sentences, 30, 34, 150, 152,
  166–167
Topics for Writing, Additional, 27,
  57, 81, 103, 127, 147, 163, 177

V

Verbs
  be, 7, 61, 67, 85, 89, 91
  correct form, 168
  irregular, 61, 85
  linking, 41
  of sentences, 4
  simple past affirmative, 85–89
  simple present affirmative, 61–67
  simple present negative, 67–68
  singular, 61, 63
  that clause and, 154, 156
Vocabulary in writing, 21, 54, 78,
  100, 124, 144, 160, 174–175
  see also Building Better Vocabulary

W

Writer's Notes
  adjective form, 40
  avoiding plagiarism, 153
  because vs. *so*, 119
  commas, 121
  going to vs. *gonna*, 107
  -ly adjectives, 93
  there are vs. *they are*, 66–67
  using *It* as a subject, 6
  writing lists of words, 70
Writing process
  editing, 25, 56–57, 80, 102, 127,
    146, 163, 172, 177
  final drafts, 172
  peer editing, 25–27, 57, 80, 102,
    127, 146, 163, 177

CREDITS

Cover © Lindrik/iStock/Getty Images

Unit 01 Page 2–3: © Anton Petrus/Moment Open/Getty Images; Page 5: © Stephen Brashear/Getty Images News/Getty Images; Page 7: © Craig Ferguson/LightRocket/Getty Images; Page 8: © Randall Scott/National Geographic Creative; Page 12: © Annie Griffiths'; Page 13: © RossHelen editorial/Alamy Stock Photo; Page 15: © The Asahi Shimbun/Getty Images; Page 23: © Xu Yuanbin/CQSB/VCG/Getty Images; Page 26: © Giuseppe Greco/REDA&CO/UIG/Getty Images

Unit 02 Page 28–29: © ALEJANDRA VEGA/AFP/Getty Images; Page 30: © James Schwabel/Alamy Stock Photo; Page 31: © DANNY HU/Moment/Getty Images; Page 34: © The Asahi Shimbun/Getty Images; Page 35: © PHILIPPE LOPEZ/AFP/Getty Images; Page 37: © Joel Van Houdt/National Geograhic Creative; Page 38: © Design pics inc/National Geographic Creative; Page 42: © Dadan Ramdani/National Geographic Creative; Page 45: © Serra Bonita; Page 50: © Sean Pavone/Alamy Stock Photo; Page 51: © Pat Greenhouse/The Boston Globe/Getty Images; Page 54: © WorldFoto/Alamy Stock Photo;

Unit 03 Page 58–59: © Asher Svidensky; Page 62: © Andreas Pein/laif/Redux; Page 64: © ROBERT HARDING PICTURE LIBRARY/National Geographic Creative; Page 66: © DESIGN PICS/National Geographic Creative; Page 72: © Danny Lawson - PA Images/Getty Images; Page 75: © Nick Gammon/Alamy Stock Photo

Unit 04 Page 82–83: © Elizabeth Daziel/National Geographic Creative; Page 86: © LongJon/Shutterstock.com; Page 87: © SAUL LOEB/AFP/Getty Images; Page 88: © Library of Congress, Prints & Photographs Division, Reproduction number LC-DIG-ggbain-12476 (digital file from original negative); Page 91: © Ben McCanna/Portland Press Herald/Getty Images; Page 100: © INTERFOTO/Alamy Stock Photo

Unit 05 Page 104–105: © Theodore Kaye; Page 107: © Hemis/Alamy Stock Photo; Page 109: © Frans Lanting/National Geographic Creative.; Page 111: © AP Images/Jason Ogulnik; Page 113: © Steven Kazlowski/Barcroft Media/Getty Images; Page 114: © REMKO DE WAAL/AFP/Getty Images; Page 118: © AP Images/Ton Koene; Page 121: © Blaine Harrington III/Alamy Stock Photo; Page 125: © David Doubilet/National Geographic Creative

Unit 06 Page 128–129: © Martin Roemers/Panos Pictures; Page 131: © VALERY HACHE/AFP/Getty Images; Page 132: © Robin Hammond/National Geographic Creative; Page 135: © Joel Sartore/National Geographic Creative; Page 137: © CHRIS J RATCLIFFE/AFP/Getty Images; Page 140: © Juniors Bildarchiv GmbH/Alamy Stock Photo; Page 141: © Frans Lanting/National Geographic Creative; Page 144: © Robert Harding Picture Library/National Geographic Creative

Unit 07 Page 148–149: © Ozgur Donmaz/DigitalVision/Getty Images; Page 151: © John S Lander/LightRocket/Getty Images; Page 152: © Ania Blazejewska/Moment/Getty Images; Page 153: © RJ Sangosti/Denver Post/Getty Images; Page 155: © Annie Griffiths; Page 162: © ALEXEY GROMOV/AFP/Getty Images

Unit 08 Page 164–165: © AP Images/Amel Emric; Page 167: © XPACIFICA/National Geographic Creative; Page 169: © redbrickstock.com/Alamy Stock Photo; Page 170: © John Gress/Corbis News/Getty Images; Page 171: © Mark Thiessen/National Geographic Magazines/Getty Images

Text Credits Page 8: Source: "Sandhya Narayanan", National Geographic. https://www.nationalgeographic.org/find-explorers/explorers/632EE4EE/sandhya-narayanan; Page 62: Source: "Hayat Sindi", National Geographic. https://www.nationalgeographic.org/find-explorers/explorers/48FC9C7F/hayat-sindi; Page 75: Source: "Pictures: Amsterdam's Lean, Green Shipping Container Homes", National Geographic. https://www.nationalgeographic.com/environment/sustainable-earth/pictures-amsterdam-shipping-container-homes/; Page 84: Source: "The Explosive Origins of the Nobel Prizes", by Juan Jose Sanchez Arreseigor, National Geographic, October 5, 2017. https://www.nationalgeographic.com/archaeology-and-history/magazine/2017/07-08/Alfred_Nobel_Founder_Prize/; Page 132: Source: "The New Europeans", by Robert Kunzig, National Geographic. https://www.nationalgeographic.com/magazine/2016/10/europe-immigration-muslim-refugees-portraits/; Page 151: Source: "Five Trends Influencing the Future of Our Cities", by Amy Kolczak, National Geographic, December 8, 2017. https://www.nationalgeographic.com/environment/urban-expeditions/green-buildings/design-trends-sustainability-cities-wellness-climate-change/; Page 152: Source: "5 Reasons the Philippines is So Disaster Prone", by Dan Vergano, National Geographic, November 11, 2013. https://news.nationalgeographic.com/news/2013/11/131111-philippines-dangers-haiyan-yolanda-death-toll-rises/?_ga=2.30901306.468041996.1523631414-1019513137.1500397993; Page 162: Source: "The Case for and Against Daylight Savings Time", by Brian Handwerk, National Geographic, November 3, 2016. https://news.nationalgeographic.com/2016/11/daylight-saving-time-2016-why-change-clocks/?_ga=2.120035275.2112246272.1522939130-1019513137.1500397993; Page 171: Source: "How Humans Are Causing Deadly Earthquakes", by Sarah Gibbens, National Geographic, October 2, 2017. https://news.nationalgeographic.com/2017/10/human-induced-earthquakes-fracking-mining-video-spd/?_ga=2.24999929.2112246272.1522939130-1019513137.1500397993; Page 175: Source: "On Island of the Colorblind, Paradise Has a Different Hue", by Daniel Stone, National Geographic, January 26, 2018. https://www.nationalgeographic.com/photography/proof/2018/01/pingelap-island-colorblindness-micronesia/; Page 105: Source: "Revolutionizing Recycling by Turning Trash into Treasure", by Cristina Nunez, National Geographic, June 2018. https://www.nationalgeographic.com/magazine/2018/06/genius-arthur-huang-plastic-waste-planet-trashpresso/?beta=true